**99 WRITING PROMPTS TO CRAFT
A TALE OF HEART AND HEROISM**

WRITE A
Romantasy

Erik Patterson
@yourdailywritingprompt

ADAMS MEDIA
New York   Amsterdam/Antwerp   London   Toronto   Sydney/Melbourne   New Delhi

adams media

Adams Media
An Imprint of Simon & Schuster, LLC
100 Technology Center Drive
Stoughton, MA 02072

For more than 100 years, Simon & Schuster has championed authors and the stories they create. By respecting the copyright of an author's intellectual property, you enable Simon & Schuster and the author to continue publishing exceptional books for years to come. We thank you for supporting the author's copyright by purchasing an authorized edition of this book.

No amount of this book may be reproduced or stored in any format, nor may it be uploaded to any website, database, language-learning model, or other repository, retrieval, or artificial intelligence system without express permission. All rights reserved. Inquiries may be directed to Simon & Schuster, 1230 Avenue of the Americas, New York, NY 10020 or permissions@simonandschuster.com.

Copyright © 2025 by Simon & Schuster, LLC

All rights reserved, including the right to reproduce this book or portions thereof in any form whatsoever. For information, address Adams Media Subsidiary Rights Department, 1230 Avenue of the Americas, New York, NY 10020.

First Adams Media trade paperback edition August 2025

ADAMS MEDIA and colophon are registered trademarks of Simon & Schuster, LLC.

Simon & Schuster strongly believes in freedom of expression and stands against censorship in all its forms. For more information, visit BooksBelong.com.

For information about special discounts for bulk purchases, please contact Simon & Schuster Special Sales at 1-866-506-1949 or business@simonandschuster.com.

The Simon & Schuster Speakers Bureau can bring authors to your live event. For more information or to book an event, contact the Simon & Schuster Speakers Bureau at 1-866-248-3049 or visit our website at www.simonspeakers.com.

Interior design by Priscilla Yuen
Images © Adobe Stock;
Simon & Schuster, LLC

Manufactured in the United States of America

1 2025

Library of Congress Cataloging-in-Publication Data has been applied for.

ISBN 978-1-5072-2503-5
ISBN 978-1-5072-2504-2 (ebook)

Many of the designations used by manufacturers and sellers to distinguish their products are claimed as trademarks. Where those designations appear in this book and Simon & Schuster, LLC, was aware of a trademark claim, the designations have been printed with initial capital letters.

Contents

Introduction 9

How to Use This Book 11

Navigate the Prompts and Trope Chapters.................... 12
The Rules 13
Start Writing 15
Putting It All Together 15

PART 1
Foundations of Romantasy · 17

Creating Your Characters 18
Worldbuilding 22

PART 2
Prompts to Inspire · 25

✒ Enemies to Lovers 26
"You're Literally the Devil" 27
"I've Never Hated Anyone More Than You" 29
"Do Me a Favor and Leave" 30
Quick Writes 32

✒ Elemental Magic 33
"You Think You Can Control Me?" 34
"Oh My God, You're on Fire" 35
"Blow Me" 37
Quick Writes 39

3

☞ Forced Proximity 40
"I Won't Let Them Find You" 41
"Don't Stand So Close to Me" 43
"We Just Have to Survive Until Tomorrow" 44
Quick Writes 46

☞ Forbidden Love 47
"You Can't Ever Tell Anyone about This" 48
"Meet Me in the Woods at Midnight" 49
"I Want Every Part of You" 51
Quick Writes 52

☞ Second Chance Romance 53
"I Can't Believe You Remember That" 54
"Maybe in Another Life" 56
"Do You Think You Can Be Different This Time?" .. 57
Quick Writes 59

☞ Friends to Lovers 60
"This Feels Impossible" 61
"Do That Thing You Always Do" 62
"I Promise I'll Never Hurt You" 64
Quick Writes 66

☞ Fairy-Tale Retellings 67
"If You Eat That, You're Gonna Regret It" 68
"I Swear This Shoe Fit Yesterday" 70
"I Don't Need You to Save Me" 72
Quick Writes 73

☞ Cozy Fantasy 74
"Coffee or Tea?" 75
"Guess What I Made for You" 77
"The Sexiest Thing You Could Do Is the Dishes" ... 79
Quick Writes 80

☞ Arranged Marriage 81
"You're Not What I Expected ... You're Better" 82
"Nope, Never, Not Now, Not Tomorrow, Not a Million
   Years from Now" 84
"Why Does It Feel Like We've Known Each Other Forever?" ... 86
Quick Writes 88

Slow Burn ... 89
"Wait, Not Yet, No, No, Okay Now" ... 90
"One Day You're Going to Love Me" ... 91
"The Wait Was Worth It" ... 93
Quick Writes ... 94

Love Triangle ... 95
"I'll Tell Her What You Told Me to Say If She Tells You" ... 96
"This Wasn't Meant for Me, Was It?" ... 97
"You Have to Make a Choice" ... 98
Quick Writes ... 100

Healthy Relationships ... 101
"Can We Talk about This?" ... 102
"I Have a Surprise for You" ... 104
"This Is All I've Ever Wanted" ... 106
Quick Writes ... 107

Mutual Pining ... 108
"They Don't Know I Exist" ... 109
"I Feel Like I Might Explode" ... 111
"Do You Think He Saw Me Staring at Him?" ... 113
Quick Writes ... 115

Only One Bed ... 116
"Close Your Eyes" ... 117
"How Did We Get Here?" ... 118
"You Stay on Your Side, I'll Stay on Mine" ... 120
Quick Writes ... 122

Only One Body ... 123
"Stop Trying to Control Me" ... 124
"Oh, That's How I Know You" ... 126
"Give Me My Body Back, You Body-Stealing Troll" ... 127
Quick Writes ... 129

Hidden Power/The Chosen One ... 130
"Everything You Need Is Here" ... 131
"Wanna See Something Special?" ... 133
"It's Time for You to Accept Who You Are" ... 134
Quick Writes ... 135

Contents + 5

☞ Time Travel 136
"It Was You" 137
"You Don't Want to Go Where I've Been" 139
"If You're Me, Then Who Am I?" 140
Quick Writes 142

☞ Meet-Cute 143
"This Must Be Yours" 144
"Do You Think It's Broken?" 146
"Haven't We Met Before?" 147
Quick Writes 149

☞ Meet-Ugly 150
"You've Got to Be Kidding Me" 151
"I Don't Hate You, I Detest You—And Yes,
   There's a Difference" 153
"Why Would You Ever Think I'd Like That?" 154
Quick Writes 156

☞ Star-Crossed Lovers 157
"Do You Believe in Destiny?" 158
"Nobody Understands Me Like You Do" 160
"Let's Leave Tonight" 162
Quick Writes 163

☞ Childhood Sweethearts 164
"It's You, It's Always Been You" 165
"You Make Me Want to Be Better Than I Am" 167
"Do You Remember the Day We Met?" 169
Quick Writes 171

☞ I Have a Secret 172
"Can I Trust You?" 173
"I'll Tell You Mine If You Tell Me Yours" 174
"Who Else Have You Told?" 175
Quick Writes 177

☞ **Fake Relationship** 178
   "I Love You, No Really" 179
   "You Thought That Was Real?" 181
   "I Didn't Know That about You" 182
   Quick Writes 184

☞ **Opposites Attract** 185
   "I Don't Feel Like Myself" 186
   "If You Think I'd Want to Be with You, You're Crazy" 188
   "Are We Really Doing This?" 190
   Quick Writes 191

☞ **Amnesia** 192
   "I'm Not Who You Think I Am" 193
   "If You Don't Stop Following Me, You're Going
      to Regret It" 195
   "Look What I Found in My Pocket" 197
   Quick Writes 199

☞ **Fish Out of Water** 200
   "I've Never Felt More Uncomfortable in
      My Entire Life" 201
   "That's Not How It Works" 203
   "I Don't Even Know Who I Am Anymore" 204
   Quick Writes 206

☞ **The Bet** 207
   "I Knew There Was Something Wrong with You" 208
   "I'm a Terrible Loser" 210
   "Can We Go Back to the Beginning?" 212
   Quick Writes 214

☞ **Just Friends** 215
   "Promise Me We'll Never Change" 216
   "I Can't Believe You Did Me Dirty Like That" 218
   "I've Got Your Back" 219
   Quick Writes 220

☛ Secret Royalty 221
"If Anyone Finds Out, I'm Ruined" 222
"Are You Telling Me What I Think You're Telling Me?" 224
"I Only Want to Be the Queen of Your Heart" 225
Quick Writes 226

☛ Found Family 227
"They Never Knew Me Like You Know Me" 228
"I Didn't Know Life Could Be So Good" 230
"Don't Worry, I've Got You" 232
Quick Writes 233

☛ Touch Her and Die 234
"You Don't Want to Test Me" 235
"I've Eaten Bigger Men for Breakfast" 237
"You'd Really Do That for Me?" 239
Quick Writes 241

☛ Stranded 242
"I Could Kill You Right Now" 243
"You're Not Gonna Like This" 245
"On the Bright Side, We're Dead" 246
Quick Writes 248

☛ Trading Places 249
"There's One Thing You Need to Know" 250
"You Better Not Destroy My Body" 251
"I'll Do It If You Will" 253
Quick Writes 255

Introduction

A frustrated romance novelist is transported into her book, where she falls in love with the scruffy rapscallion pirate she created.

A powerless enchantress aligns herself with a human thief; together they fight the gods to restore peace to their kingdom.

An angel hiding among humans works an office job to fit in. When her identity is revealed, her new love interest and friends are in danger.

Intrigued? That's the magical pull of romantasy. If you create rich characters, put them in a fantastical world filled with spells, mythical lore, and mystical creatures, and add romantic yearnings, you'll have your readers hooked from page one. *Write a Romantasy* will launch you on that writing path.

Whether you've written a romantasy before and just want to generate new ideas or this is your first time writing in this genre, expect to learn new tips and tools for setting up your story's world, characters, and plot. You'll use the first part of this book to create the foundation of your romantasy universe and identify the core fantasy elements you plan to incorporate. These otherworldly details are integral to the romantasy subgenre. It's important to have fun with them!

Part 2 of this book will help you map out your plot and develop your characters. Here, you'll find thirty-three chapters organized by romance trope (a common theme or literary device), such as the Meet-Cute, Second

Chance Romance, Slow Burn, and others. You'll explore each trope through a number of prompts that will help you define your characters and their relationships—everything from why they are drawn to each other (or torn apart), what hurdles they must overcome for their love, and how to make their chemistry sizzle. Ultimately, each of the ninety-nine prompts will thrust you forward in your story, helping you brainstorm ideas and develop scenes and chapters. For example:

- Learn how to build conflict between enemies who will eventually become lovers.
- Recycle ideas that are hundreds of years old (from fairy tales, for example) and make them feel new again.
- Broaden your characters' perspectives by having them switch bodies with another character or lose their memory entirely.
- And more!

Remember: You're limited only by the boundaries of your own imagination. Your characters can be anyone, your romantasy can take place anywhere. And just because a prompt inspires you to write a new scene does not mean it *must* end up in your final draft. Sometimes the whole point of writing a scene is simply to gain a deeper understanding of your own characters as you're creating them. So, whether you're writing a novel, fan fiction, screenplay, short story, RPG campaign, or comic, be bold! Good storytelling is all about taking risks. Silence those dating apps, cast a productivity spell, and get started!

How to Use This Book

Romantasy is a subgenre of fantasy and romance—a romance-driven plot in a fantasy world. It's popular among readers and writers alike because it offers an escape from the pressures of the real world. Romantasy combines the most compelling parts of both genres, captivating readers with daring adventures and magical love stories. The best romantasy books take you to a world you want to visit again and again.

If your favorite romantasy books completely enthrall you, you're destined to become obsessed with these writing exercises too. This opening section of *Write a Romantasy* illustrates how you can best use these prompts: First, you'll find a detailed description of how each prompt works and how the prompts can provide a structure to your writing sessions. Then, before you start writing, you'll get a taste of some rules. You'll also learn some pointers on starting the writing process, and finish up with suggestions on how to tie everything together. But first, let's think about what makes up a trope and why this book is built around them.

👉 Navigate the Prompts and Trope Chapters

If you're writing romantasy, chances are you're a romantasy reader. So, you know how passionately readers feel about tropes. For the uninitiated, a trope is a common plot device that readers recognize from other stories. The familiarity is a feature, not a bug. Readers seek out their favorite Arranged Marriage stories; they argue what's more satisfying, Friends to Lovers or Enemies to Lovers; they obsessively debate how slowly a Slow Burn romantasy should progress. Romantasy readers are faithful to tropes they adore.

Which is why each of the prompts in this book is grounded in a romantasy trope. And just as a Love Triangle can end in a "why not both" decision, committing to only one trope is not necessary. Your story might start with a Meet-Cute that leads to Mutual Pining that gets interrupted by Amnesia that then gets complicated by Only One Bed. Your challenge as a writer is to find ways to subvert these tropes and make them feel fresh again.

Every prompt is broken into several parts: The Scenario section gives you a basic setup for your scene. These scenarios aren't set in stone—feel free to change details to make them fit your story. The Brainstorm section poses questions to limber up your imagination and get you prepared for situations that might come up as you write. The Write section is the actual prompt. Then the remaining sections give you more ideas to explore. And don't forget, each prompt title works as a line of dialogue that can serve as a jumping-off point when you're writing. Start with that line and see what comes next, or use the line wherever it fits best.

Each chapter features three longer prompts followed by five additional Quick Write prompts. These five prompts ask you to write continuously for 15 minutes without editing or censoring yourself. You may use these prompts at any point throughout your writing process. They're especially useful for getting into a groove at the beginning of a longer writing sprint.

Now that you have a better idea of how to approach the prompts in this book, let's establish some writing romantasy rules. These rules are going to become a vital element of your writing process that you can come back to again and again whenever you feel creatively stuck.

👉 The Rules

Before you start writing, let's establish a set of rules for your romantasy writing practice. The goal of each rule is to fuel your creative fire and unlock that passion on the page.

RULE 1 — These rules are meant to be broken.

There's no one way to write something. If someone tells you there is, they're wrong. Especially when it comes to romantasy, where a Prince of Darkness and Queen of Light can fall madly in love, or a cursed sword can interrupt a couple's transformation from friends to lovers by sending them on a dangerous quest in a demonic dimension, or a giant bounty hunter can be captured by a flirtatious pickpocketing elf. Anything goes when you're writing a romantasy.

RULE 2 — Think big.

Sometimes prompt books don't leave enough room for your imagination. Here's a prompt you won't find in this book: "A heartbroken werewolf gets injured outside a widow's cottage and this unlikely pair falls in love as the widow nurses the werewolf back to health." It's too specific. What if you want to write about a time-traveling lothario, a witch who's lost her powers, or a goddess who travels across galaxies to find the human lover she once banished to another land? Your eyes would glaze over at this werewolf prompt. Whereas "your protagonist gets injured outside a stranger's cottage, and they fall in love as the stranger nurses your protagonist back to health" allows you to fill in the blanks and make the prompt your own.

Which is why you'll see broader character signifiers here: protagonist, antagonist, friend, lover, etc. Instead of telling you exactly what to write, these prompts will guide you toward your best creative impulses.

RULE 3 — Write badly.

It doesn't have to come out perfectly the first time. Trying to make it "good" gets in the way of getting it down. Just write. You can make it better later.

RULE 4   Do it again.

These prompts are not intended to be one-and-done. Do them over and over and what you write will be different every time. Hopefully, you'll use this book for the rest of your life.

RULE 5   Use what works for you.

These prompts are designed to get you writing. Go all in or just go with whatever parts of a prompt move you and ignore the parts that don't. If a prompt seems too specific, feel free to modify it or focus on the elements you find most inspiring. Don't twist yourself into a pretzel trying to respond to every aspect of a prompt. You aren't being graded, so there's no such thing as getting the prompt wrong. Same goes for pronouns. If a prompt says "she" and your character is a "he" or a "they," default to your character's pronouns.

RULE 6   Use the headers as jumping-off points.

Each prompt's header is a line of dialogue. Try to work these lines into your writing. But don't worry about being exact—you can tweak the line to fit your scene. These dialogue prompts can be first lines, or you can build toward them. You're in charge.

RULE 7   Hold yourself accountable.

The hardest part of writing is sometimes just keeping yourself accountable; try to do at least one prompt a day. You'll be amazed by the progress you make when you write daily, even for a short time. Set a timer for 20–40 minutes, then put your phone on the other side of the room. Focus on the prompt until the timer goes off.

These rules are important, but follow them with a grain of salt—remember Rule 1! Now that you have some guidelines on how to approach the writing process, it's time to start writing your romantasy!

👉 Start Writing

Now grab a notebook, or open up a new document on your computer, and get busy. If you already have an outline, look for prompts that address specific needs in your story. If you're not planning to outline or need help finding a story to tell, pick a trope you love, go to that chapter, and start there. And if you're struggling with writer's block, pick a prompt at random—they can be done in any order, and there's no limit to how many prompts you use. Whenever you're stuck, a new prompt will get you going again.

👉 Putting It All Together

Here's a secret: The process of writing can be as thrilling as romantasy. Just as your characters are going on an adventure, you're embarking on one as the writer too. Think of the characters you invent in the Creating Your Characters section and the setting you establish in the Worldbuilding section as your means of travel; then all the scenes you write using the prompts that follow are like the various destinations on your writing trip's itinerary. The prompts in this book can help you experience the joy of letting your imagination go and discovering what happens on the page.

Whether you meticulously plot out your story using an outline, allow it to unfold organically as you write, revise using sticky notes to move plot points and details around, or do something entirely different, putting it all together looks unique for everyone. You'll cement your story's world and characters in Part 1 of *Write a Romantasy*, then combine them with the conflicts and plot points you'll dream up in Part 2. You can always shift scenes around to find the ideal order and add details as you revise, so you send your characters on a complicated journey where they flourish, regress, fight for their love, or get totally heartbroken—not necessarily in that order. This book gives you a framework to create the ultimate romantasy. You are the only person who can write this story using your unique voice. So, write it.

PART 1
FOUNDATIONS
of
ROMANTASY

YOUR JOB AS A ROMANTASY WRITER IS TWOFOLD: Create indelible characters who capture your readers' hearts and build a compelling world that engages their imaginations. This introductory section to *Write a Romantasy* is your road map to accomplishing both goals.

There's been much debate about what makes a "true" romantasy: If the primary stakes are romantic and the fantasy elements are secondary, does that qualify? What if the will-they-or-won't-they aspect of your central relationship takes a back seat to the adventure? Ideally, you'll find a balance between both, but it's okay if you favor one element over the other. You're still writing romantasy; don't let anyone tell you otherwise.

The way you blend romance with fantasy is the magic potion that makes your romantasy unique. Just remember: It's your characters who take your readers on this journey, so make sure they have what it takes to drive the story. The Character Creation Cheat Sheet in the following pages will help you clarify how your characters behave romantically and what heroic qualities they possess.

Next you will find tools for building the fantasy world of your story. Pick a setting and answer the questions in the Worldbuilding Questionnaire. Do this a few times, and imagine the challenges your characters face in these new fantasy worlds. This is how your story comes to life.

☞ Creating Your Characters

Think about how complicated you are.

Everyone has secrets, hopes, dreams, passions, regrets, triumphs. If you mapped out all the traits that make you unique and interesting, you'd probably find that you would make a good character in a book. Write someone who has as many layers as you do, but with even bigger secrets, more urgent hopes, more passionate dreams, deeper regrets, and more thrilling triumphs. Everything is heightened in romantasy, so let your characters be more extreme versions of people you might meet in the real world.

You might already have a million romantasy characters in your head, but whenever you need inspiration, use this Character Creation Cheat Sheet. Just select an Archetype—which is essentially a universally recognized character type—from the following section, and one or two adjectives from the list of Prime Characteristics. And if you don't want your character to be human, choose a Fantasy Type. It's a simple formula:

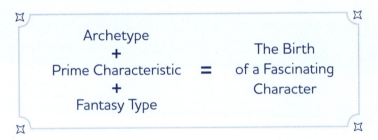

Use this formula to create as many romantasy characters as you want. Mix and match for variety!

Archetypes

Every romantasy has a hero or a heroine, but there are several different types of characters that are so ingrained in storytelling traditions that your readers will both recognize them and expect to see them. Think of these Archetypes as the foundation for the characters you create.

Hero/Heroine: A character who must go on a journey. They often have hidden powers, and they will be transformed by love. They want more from life than they currently have. They have flaws and room for growth.

Love Interest: The love interest often begins as a foil, helping your readers to see your protagonist more clearly. This character's hidden depths only become transparent as they get to know your protagonist.

Best Friend/Ally: A sounding board for your hero/heroine, but they often have a romantic journey of their own. They either get your protagonist out of trouble or complicate the drama.

Mentor: Your protagonist will need help on their journey—their mentor is often an older, perhaps magical and enigmatic, character who can set them on the right path and guide them along the way.

Villain/Foil: Your antagonist will create conflict for your protagonist, making it difficult for them to complete their journey. They want things like power, revenge, and control.

Comedic Relief: A comedic foil for your protagonist. They can be friend or foe.

The Trickster: Deceitful without being malicious. They love stirring up trouble.

Reluctant Warrior: Though they'd prefer to remain home and avoid conflict, they are the only one powerful enough to conquer an enemy. They will ultimately choose to save the world.

The Betrayer/Rebel: They never do what they're told. When they commit heroic acts, they do so reluctantly because it's the right thing to do and they have a moral code.

Prime Characteristics

Your characters might exhibit any of these traits at different points in your story. But you can define who they are at their core with one or two characteristics from this list. Think of it as their default settings.

ABRASIVE	DUTIFUL	KLUTZY	RESILIENT
AGGRESSIVE	EAGER	KOOKY	RESTLESS
AMBITIOUS	EDUCATED	LOGICAL	SELF-CENTERED
AMORAL	EMOTIONAL	LOVING	SELFLESS
ANXIOUS	ENTHUSIASTIC	LOYAL	SENSITIVE
ATHLETIC	FAIR	MANIPULATIVE	SHREWD
BENEVOLENT	FAITHFUL	MINDFUL	SKEPTICAL
BLUNT	FEARLESS	MODEST	SMUG
BOLD	FRIENDLY	NAIVE	SPIRITUAL
BRAVE	FRIVOLOUS	NOBLE	STOIC
CARING	GENEROUS	NURTURING	STUBBORN
CAUTIOUS	GENTLE	OBEDIENT	TENACIOUS
CHARISMATIC	HAPPY	OBSERVANT	THOUGHTFUL
CHEERFUL	HARDWORKING	OPTIMISTIC	TIDY
CLEARHEADED	HARSH	ORDERLY	TRUSTING
CLEVER	HONEST	PERSISTENT	VALIANT
COMPASSIONATE	IDEALISTIC	PERSUASIVE	VICIOUS
COMPETITIVE	IMPETUOUS	POSITIVE	VIRTUOUS
CONFIDENT	INDEPENDENT	PRACTICAL	VISIONARY
CRAFTY	INTUITIVE	QUIET	WHIMSICAL
CURIOUS	JADED	QUIRKY	WISE
DARING	JEALOUS	QUIXOTIC	WITTY
DECEPTIVE	JITTERY	RECKLESS	ZANY
DECISIVE	KIND	RELIABLE	ZEALOUS

Fantasy Types

When it comes to romantasy, your characters can come from endless backgrounds and play various roles in society. Use this list of types to create a diverse cast of characters.

ALIEN	ELF	MAGICIAN	SLAYER
ANDROID	FAIRY	MERMAID	SPIRIT
ANGEL	GHOST	NECROMANCER	SPY
ASSASSIN	GIANT	ORC	SUPERHERO
BARD	GNOME	ORPHAN	TRICKSTER
BEAST	GOBLIN	PIRATE	TROLL
CENTAUR	GOD	PRIEST	UNICORN
CHANGELING	HALFLING	PRINCESS	VAMPIRE
CHOSEN ONE	HEALER	REBEL	VIKING
CYCLOPS	HUMAN	SATYR	WARRIOR
DEVIL	HUNTER	SEER	WEREWOLF
DRAGON	IMP	SHIFTER	ZOMBIE
DRUID	INCUBUS	SHOPKEEPER	

As you build your characters, experiment with different combinations of Archetypes, Prime Characteristics, and Fantasy Types. Before you settle on who your protagonist is, you might want to imagine different versions of them in the world you'll create in the next section, as the details of this world might help determine the types of characters you see living there.

☛ Worldbuilding

When are you done building a world?

Honestly, never. But that's a good thing!

Worldbuilding is a constantly evolving process. You will be building your romantasy world until the day your book is published—and even then, you won't be done. If you're writing a book series, you still have boundless corners of your world to uncover. But even if this is a one-and-done book, the world you create will be so real to you that it'll keep expanding in your head for the rest of your life. This is both the blessing and the curse of being a writer. Thankfully, it's more blessing than curse!

The world of your romantasy might have shades and echoes of the world we live in now, but with a fantastical edge to it. Your story might take place on Earth in the year 3056, deep in the ocean, in a cave community, in a futuristic city, in a magical realm, in another galaxy, in ancient Rome, in a domain overrun by dragons, in a desert landscape, in a mystical faery universe, or in a fallen kingdom. The key to building a world readers want to come back to, again and again, is in the details.

▶ Types of Worlds ◀

Romantasy can be divided into subgenres with different vibes and visual landscapes. Find the genre in the following list that most closely matches what you're writing, then use one of the suggested settings as a jumping-off point for the first scene in your story.

Dystopian Romantasy: Your world looks like the modern world in decay. Your story unfolds in a near future that has taken a catastrophic turn. Potential Starter Settings: a desolate town, a fallout shelter, a crumbling city.

High Romantasy: Your world is fantastical. It is populated by mythical creatures, and the universe is guided by magical systems. Potential Starter Settings: a cave inhabited by dragons, an enchanted forest, a pirate cove.

Magical Realism: Your world looks like the real world and feels grounded, but with subtle fantastical differences. Your story contains spells, magic, and potions. Potential Starter Settings: a secluded valley, a quaint home with a hidden passage that leads to a secret room, a witch's hideout.

Paranormal Romantasy: Your world is inhabited by ghosts, ghouls, and creatures that wake you up in the middle of the night. Potential Starter Settings: a haunted house, a vampire's underground lair, a werewolf den.

Sci-Fi Romantasy: Your world is a blend of science fiction, fantasy, and romance. Your story might take place in space or other worlds with aliens and androids. Potential Starter Settings: a shuttle nearing its final destination, an underground citadel, a pristine white room.

Sword and Sorcery: Your world is full of sword-wielding heroes, witchy villains, and mysterious magical friends. Your story is most likely set in the past. Potential Starter Settings: a fall faire, the town center before a beheading, the Queen's bedroom.

Urban Romantasy: Your world is gritty and dark, with fantasy elements. Your story takes place in a city with skyscrapers, and your lovers probably meet at work. Potential Starter Settings: a boardroom, a building rooftop with a starry sky overhead, a monolithic structure that is cursed.

Try this to help you get started:

Write down everything you know about the world you're creating. Wherever you are, whenever an idea pops into your head, write it down.

Worldbuilding Questionnaire

The questions on this list are designed to get you thinking about how deep and complex the world of your story can be. Use these questions to begin exploring what your world looks like, but don't feel limited by this list. Follow any paths these questions send you down.

- Using your senses, how would you describe the world around you? How does it look, sound, smell, taste, and feel?
- What initial emotional responses does this world elicit from you? Why?
- What do people (or creatures) wear in this world? How do they wear their hair (if they have any)?
- What are the culinary delicacies of this world, and what are the most romantic spots where your characters might go to eat, drink, and dance?

- What's the most dangerous thing about this world? What activities are illegal? And how might this atmosphere impact the lovers in your story?
- What common self-care practices are popular in this world?
- What is the most common language? What other means of communication do people use beyond language? How do lovers communicate when they're apart?
- What does it mean to be rich here? How do lower-class people survive? How do these financial hierarchies affect romantic relationships?
- What is the ultimate sign of success? How are heroes rewarded?
- What behavior is considered inappropriate?
- What does a single person's home look like? Describe it from the outside, then from the inside. How does it differ from a typical family home?
- What do people do for entertainment and recreation? Describe a typical date night here.
- List five things that people would find surprising about this world.
- List five reasons why you would want to live here. Then, list five reasons why you'd hate living here.

Feel free to add your own questions to this list.

This world is inside you, and you'll continue to define what it looks and feels like as you get deeper into your story, so don't get too bogged down by prewriting. You have your characters, and you've begun building the foundation of the world of your story. Now it's time to explore the prompts in the rest of this book and start writing!

PART 2
Prompts *to* Inspire

IN THIS SECTION OF THE BOOK, you'll find a plethora of writing prompts tailored for the romantasy tropes readers love most. Each prompt has several ideas to help you develop characters, map out their journeys, and get started on new scenes. In addition, the Quick Write prompts provide extra jumping-off points. These can be especially useful at the start of a writing session.

Now, let go of any preconceived ideas or expectations as you dive into each prompt. Just write. You'll feel your creative engine warming up, and by the time you finish, your synapses will be firing at sixty thoughts a minute. Keep writing and see where those thoughts take you.

These prompts are fuel for your creative engine. You're in charge of how you use them. They are designed to inspire—to unleash your passion for romantasy and keep the words flowing until you've brought an entirely new world of wonder and love to life.

Enemies to Lovers

Stories where two characters begin as antagonists but ultimately find themselves in a romantic relationship are always full of extreme emotions. There's no mistaking when they are on the path from Enemies to Lovers. The animosity between them might be ancient. Maybe they've despised each other since childhood. Or maybe they met in adulthood, and it was hate at first sight.

A power imbalance—boss/employee, god/human, royalty/peasant—might have fostered their hostility. Or they might come from wildly different backgrounds and can't imagine how they could ever see eye to eye. Perhaps they're in competition, vying for the same promotion or both trying to get the last available seat on an intergalactic shuttle of pioneers destined to settle on a faraway planet. They've wronged each other in many ways and the wounds are deep.

However their hatred was born, it feels like an insurmountable obstacle. These two characters will clash. But the inciting incident (a pivotal event that sets the story in motion) will unite them against their will. They will be partnered in some way, forced to work together, possibly for their very survival.

The icy chill between them will thaw. They will discover unknown similarities; they will be vulnerable; they will begin to bond. Ultimately, they'll realize they can't live without each other.

"You're Literally the Devil"

◆ SCENARIO ◆

Your protagonist could never see herself with this person. *Ever.* They have a long, complicated history of disagreements and fights. There's no way she could hate this person more than she already does. At least that's what she thought, but then she finds out this person isn't who he says he is.

◆ BRAINSTORM ◆

What's the most dramatic way for her to discover the truth? Come up with ten possible ways this scene could play out, even if some of the ideas are terrible. (Get your bad ideas out of the way to find the better ones.)

Think about the enemy's secret. What are his motivations for keeping it hidden?

◆ WRITE ◆

Write a scene where your protagonist finds out what her enemy has been hiding. The truth about who he is and what he's done. The pain he has caused.

Give her a moment where she confronts him and unleashes all her fury. Think of it as an emotional aria. Make her pain palpable. She didn't know she could feel so deeply. Give him a moment where he expresses genuine remorse. Does this change the way she sees him?

Remember: The hate between these characters is shallow. Think about how you can use the depth of your protagonist's emotion here to clue readers into the fact that she does care for him.

◆ OPTIONAL ELEMENTS TO INCLUDE ◆

- A moment where her enemy tries to convince her that his secret isn't that bad.
- A moment of physical contact.
- Another character overhearing their argument.

Fantasy Twist

After you've written a draft of your scene, read through it and look for places where you can elevate the fantastical elements of this world. Do your characters have powers? Does their ability to use these powers change when they feel love versus hate?

"I've Never Hated Anyone More Than You"

◆ SCENARIO ◆

Your protagonist and her enemy are developing feelings for each other, but they haven't expressed or acted on them. That's going to change today.

◆ BRAINSTORM ◆

Before you start writing, list at least ten things your protagonist hates about the other person. Then, list at least ten things your protagonist loves about the other person. Use these details as she describes how conflicted she's feeling in the scene you write.

◆ WRITE ◆

Write a scene that begins as an argument and becomes a confession of love. Start with the line "I've never hated anyone more than you." Then build to a "but . . ."

"But I can't stop thinking about you."
"But I don't know who I am anymore."
"But I also love you."

Begin with the fight, then get to the "but" later in the scene. Earn the "but."

Remember: Think of their fight as a sporting match. How many points do they each score?

◆ OPTIONAL ELEMENTS TO INCLUDE ◆

- A moment of levitation, either literal or metaphorical.
- A small lie (to create drama later in your story).
- A moment of disbelief.

Fantasy Twist

What if this was a dream, or a vision, or a nightmare? How would that change the arc of the scene?

" Do Me a Favor and Leave "

◆ SCENARIO ◆

Your characters have consummated their relationship. They've moved past enemies into the lovers stage. Things are going well. But then your protagonist backslides. She momentarily forgets how much they've been through and reverts to her old self, the one who hated this guy's guts. She says something that hurts him.

◆ BRAINSTORM ◆

What's the worst thing she could do to her lover? Make a quick list of betrayals, from kinda bad to terrible. Don't censor yourself. Even if it feels unforgiveable, put it on your list. When you have at least ten ideas, circle the ones that feel like they have the most energy. Then do some freewriting about how her lover might react to these offenses.

◆ WRITE ◆

Write a scene where your protagonist reverts to her former self. She makes a huge mistake and either says or does something cruel to her lover. These words wouldn't have hurt him before, but now it feels like a knife to the heart. He asks her to leave. What actions can she take to make it right again?

Remember: They've seen each other at their worst, but they've also been incredibly vulnerable with each other. It might look like there's no coming back from this betrayal—but in the end, their love for each other will prevail. Let this be a fallout that ultimately brings them closer together.

◆ OPTIONAL ELEMENTS TO INCLUDE ◆

- Your protagonist drops to the floor.
- Uncomfortable fidgeting.
- A promise taken back.

Fantasy Twist

In your story's unique world, what additional obstacles can you create to make it more difficult for your protagonist to win back her lover's heart? What if he retreats to a location where she can't physically go, or she's forbidden to go?

Callbacks

Look at earlier fight scenes you've already written between these two characters. Find a line that you can echo in this scene, but it has a totally different meaning at this point in their relationship. Make it ache to see them back in this place again.

Quick Writes

Set a timer for 15 minutes and do not stop writing until the timer goes off. Do not edit, cross out, or censor yourself. Write down every thought that comes to you.

1. Write a scene where your protagonist tries to sabotage her enemy. What are the worst possible things your protagonist could do?
2. Write a scene where the enemy overhears your protagonist telling a friend how much he's hurt her.
3. Write a scene where your protagonist destroys something her enemy loves. This is something she'll never be able to fix.
4. Write a scene where your protagonist learns about a traumatic event from her enemy's childhood.
5. Write a scene where your protagonist fixes something her enemy broke, and a small, tentative connection begins to form.

Elemental Magic

Characters with Elemental Magic can reshape the earth, bend the air, walk on water, and set the world on fire . . . literally. All their special abilities are connected to nature. They can manipulate the environment in enchanting, thrilling, and scary ways.

With this type of magic, you have a lot of questions to ask and answer. Where do they get their powers? In what ways do their powers change how they relate to others? How much self-control do they have and what happens when they go too far? You make the final call. They may have been born with magical abilities, or you might have them discover their powers during your story. As their journey progresses, they become more comfortable in their supernatural skin.

You don't have to stick to the four classical elements— earth, air, water, fire—when you're writing characters with Elemental Magic. Your characters might control metal, gas, lightning, shadows, chemicals, glass, or molecular atoms. They could even manipulate elements of your own invention. Why limit yourself to the elements that exist in the real world when you can let your imagination run free?

Most importantly, since you're writing romantasy, don't forget steam, as in: How might your characters use their magical abilities in their most private, sexy moments? This is a chance to create off-the-charts chemistry. Have fun with it.

"You Think You Can Control Me?"

◆ SCENARIO ◆

Your protagonist and her love interest both like being in charge, and they both have Elemental Magic. They would never use their powers against each other. Or would they?

◆ BRAINSTORM ◆

How do your protagonist's powers work? Come up with five rules about the nature of her powers. Do the same thing for her love interest, who might have different powers to make the chemistry between them more volatile.

◆ WRITE ◆

Write a scene that begins with a small fight between your protagonist and her love interest. But the more they get into it, the more heated they become. Until one of them is pushed to a boiling point—and they use their powers. The fight moves beyond words into full-on superpower chaos. What does this look like? Include every juicy detail.

Remember: These two characters love each other. They don't *want* to physically hurt each other. Add a moment where you show they're secretly holding back.

◆ OPTIONAL ELEMENTS TO INCLUDE ◆

- The destruction of public property.
- A secret, revealed.
- An apology.

Fantasy Twist

What is the social hierarchy in this world? If there's a class system, think about where people with Elemental Magic rank. How much social influence and power do they hold? Do they answer to anyone?

"Oh My God, You're on Fire"

◆ SCENARIO ◆

Your protagonist doesn't want anyone to know about her powers. Either she's keeping her abilities secret to protect herself from enemies, or she just isn't ready for the world to know what she can do. But her powers are about to come out . . . by accident.

◆ BRAINSTORM ◆

Who has your protagonist confided in before this scene? Does her lover know, and if so, how did he react? Who else knows about her powers? Who does she trust most? Come up with a backstory about a time when she revealed her powers to someone she trusted and it went badly. Hurtful, hateful things were said. Words that still echo through your protagonist's head.

No matter how hard she tries to let go of this moment from her past, the wound feels fresh. She knows she could be more open and trusting with her lover if she could only get past this. Freewrite about what it would take for her to get closure and heal.

◆ WRITE ◆

Write a scene where your protagonist has a huge win. This is something she's been working toward for a long time, and it's finally happened! But while she's in the middle of publicly celebrating, she loses control of her emotions . . . and she inadvertently displays her powers. How do people react? What does your protagonist do after being exposed? Does her lover help in any way?

Remember: Ultimately, you want your protagonist to embrace her powers. This is one step in her journey. Think about how this accidental coming-out can ultimately be a good thing for her. Maybe her lover helps her get to this moment of acceptance?

◆ OPTIONAL ELEMENTS TO INCLUDE ◆

- A scream.
- Someone's hair catches fire.
- A moment of confusion, when your protagonist doesn't know why other people are afraid because she doesn't yet realize she's exhibited her powers.

Callbacks

How can this scene echo the rejection from your protagonist's past? What old emotions come back up? Draw some parallels between her old trauma and this new incident.

"Blow Me"

◆ SCENARIO ◆

Your protagonist is on a long journey with a group of travelers. She's holed up at an inn for the night. She's exhausted and hungry, but also, let's face it, horny. There's one person in the group she has her eyes on. He's smart and funny, and there seems to be mutual attraction. Neither of them knows they both have Elemental Magic powers.

◆ BRAINSTORM ◆

Does your protagonist ever use her powers to "turn up the heat" during sex? What happens when two people with fire powers hook up? Or two people with water powers? Or two people who can control air? Do their powers intensify? Is there any danger in two such powerful people getting together? What if their combined energy causes a natural disaster? And more importantly, in the heat of the moment, do they even care?

◆ WRITE ◆

Write a scene where your protagonist is getting ready to go to bed, but then she changes her mind. She invites her love interest down to the bar for drinks instead. One drink turns into two, which turns into three. Soon they're trying to impress each other by showing off their individual powers. See how long you can tease your readers with this mischievous foreplay before they finally head up to one of their rooms.

◆ OPTIONAL ELEMENTS TO INCLUDE ◆

- ◆ A burnt shirt.
- ◆ A broken bed.
- ◆ Too much alcohol.
- ◆ A moment where your protagonist feels the most intense joy she has ever experienced in her life.
- ◆ A moment of laughter.

Fantasy Twist

What if two powerful beings hooking up causes their powers to change? Write a morning-after scene where your protagonist discovers her powers aren't working right. Think about how this shift in power colors your protagonist's feelings about last night. She had a great time... but now maybe she isn't so sure. Can she take it back?

Quick Writes

Set a timer for 15 minutes and do not stop writing until the timer goes off. Do not edit, cross out, or censor yourself. Write down every thought that comes to you.

1. Write a scene where your protagonist underestimates her own strength and accidentally endangers a group of people she's trying to save. When her lover tries to help, does she accept his assistance or turn him away?

2. Write a scene where disastrous weather traps two characters together. One secretly has the power to shift the weather, but they don't want to miss this opportunity for connection.

3. Write a scene where your protagonist tends to her lover's wound. Your protagonist doesn't have the medical supplies she needs, but she's able to improvise and provide medical care.

4. Write a scene where your protagonist must perform an elaborate spell that incorporates at least two natural elements. The spell does not work the way she intended.

5. Write a spicy scene where your characters get passionate in the middle of a storm. Play with how the storm mirrors their emotions; perhaps it intensifies as their physical connection grows.

Forced Proximity

*I*f you visited a thousand different parallel universes and checked in on these two characters, you might find them in a relationship in only *one* of those universes. In the rest, they never would've met. They probably come from different socioeconomic backgrounds, have different interests, and have opposing belief systems. At first glance, you'd never expect them to fall in love.

Then they're thrown together by circumstances beyond their control. Their Forced Proximity could happen in many ways. They might be assigned the same cubicle at work or be partnered up at school. Or they're imprisoned in the same cell. Or they're accidentally cuffed together without a key.

At first, there's tension; neither of them wants to be there. It's easy to focus on someone's flaws when you're too close for comfort. But then they're shocked to discover their differences are bringing them closer to each other. It's like their worlds are expanding. Ultimately, they go from dreading their time together to craving it. The fun of a Forced Proximity story is teasing your readers with this evolution. Readers should see what's coming before your characters do.

Whatever scenario you create to bring these two characters together, make it a situation they can't easily get out of. The closer their quarters, the higher the stakes. Make them squirm before you let them realize this other person isn't so bad after all.

"I Won't Let Them Find You"

◆ SCENARIO ◆

Your protagonist is running from someone: a violent former lover, a deranged ex–best friend, the police (maybe she's wanted for a crime she didn't commit), or a jealous god. She's relocated, changed her identity, and altered her appearance. Then she does something she said she'd never do—open her heart up to someone new. Is love worth the risk?

◆ BRAINSTORM ◆

What would happen to your protagonist if she got caught? The stakes should be as high as possible. There's a reason she's running—make us feel it.

Think about the person who's chasing her. Does her enemy have a reputation? What are the worst things her enemy has ever done? Why do they want your protagonist so badly? Now think about the love interest. Come up with three reasons why your protagonist finds him trustworthy.

◆ WRITE ◆

Write a scene where your protagonist and her love interest get trapped in a space so small it's hard to avoid touching. The longer they're stuck, the closer they get. Both physically and emotionally. He knows she's afraid of something, or someone. So, he asks what she's running from. And she tells him everything.

Remember: This is the moment where the love interest decides to stay or run. (Metaphorically, at least—they're still stuck together.) His reaction is key. Your protagonist is about to find out what he's made of. Will he be there when she needs him most?

◆ OPTIONAL ELEMENTS TO INCLUDE ◆

- A lie.
- Your protagonist asks the love interest to scratch an itch she can't reach.
- An unexpected but welcome (and consensual) kiss.

Fantasy Twist

What if whoever your protagonist is running from isn't human? What if they aren't even from this world? What if she isn't even quite sure what her enemy is capable of? How does this change the stakes of this scene?

"Don't Stand So Close to Me"

◆ SCENARIO ◆

Your protagonist must defeat her enemy. She won't be able to do it alone, so she partners with her enemy's enemy—whom she can't stand. The only reason she's spending time with him is because she needs him.

◆ BRAINSTORM ◆

What makes this guy so bad? Make a list of fifty reasons why your protagonist finds him repulsive. Yes, *fifty* reasons! Some of these reasons are going to be a stretch. She hates him because of his relationship with her enemy, but she'll eventually learn he isn't the bad guy she thought he was.

◆ WRITE ◆

Write a scene where your protagonist and her tentative ally are hiding out together, staking out the enemy's hideout. They're waiting for their enemy to show their face so they can confront them. But they end up waiting for a long, long time. And they can't stop bickering.

◆ OPTIONAL ELEMENTS TO INCLUDE ◆

- They share a sweet treat.
- Their knees touch.
- It begins to rain.

Fantasy Twist

What if your protagonist could read minds? Write a scene where she hears her tentative ally thinking something bad about her. Mortified, she stops listening. But whatever she heard, she got it wrong. He's into her, but she stopped listening too soon to learn that.

"We Just Have to Survive Until Tomorrow"

◆ SCENARIO ◆

Your protagonist is on some sort of retreat with a coworker she can't stand. An unexpected storm comes up and they get trapped. They are forced to rely on each other in a dangerous situation where they're each other's only hope for survival.

◆ BRAINSTORM ◆

Is your protagonist the type of person others go to in emergencies? What about her coworker? Think about all the ways in which these two characters are different. If he is salt, she is pepper. If she is day, he is night. Make a long list of their differences.

◆ WRITE ◆

Your protagonist and her coworker have been stuck at this retreat for several days. They are running out of food and water. They don't know if they're ever going to get out of here. Write a scene where the coworker tries to convince your protagonist not to give up. Show your readers his soft side. Make us fall in love with him because of how gentle and caring he is. He puts your protagonist first. He makes her feel like tomorrow is a possibility.

Remember: Your protagonist thinks she can't make a relationship work with her coworker. But she's wrong. What are the reasons they're right for each other that your protagonist just doesn't see yet?

◆ OPTIONAL ELEMENTS TO INCLUDE ◆

- A panic attack.
- A moment where he takes her in his arms to comfort her.
- The discovery of a secret passageway.

Fantasy Twist

What if this retreat is taking place on another planet? How might the atmosphere and terrain of this planet make it even more dangerous for your protagonist and her coworker to be stuck here?

Callbacks

What was the relationship between these colleagues like at the beginning of this retreat compared to where they are now? Your protagonist might reference how much they've both changed.

Quick Writes

Set a timer for 15 minutes and do not stop writing until the timer goes off. Do not edit, cross out, or censor yourself. Write down every thought that comes to you.

1. Write a scene where your protagonist is trapped in a coffin with a crush who doesn't know how she feels. Your protagonist does ridiculous things to avoid revealing how much she enjoys being so close.

2. Write a scene where your protagonist is imprisoned in an unfamiliar world. She's stuck in a cell with a stranger who teaches her the customs of this planet. And in a short time, your protagonist begins to depend on him. What feelings does this lead to?

3. Your protagonist is on a long journey in a small vehicle (anything from a tiny car to a claustrophobic spaceship) with her biggest rival. Write a scene where they share stories about their childhoods, and she discovers they aren't as different as she thought.

4. Your protagonist is being forced to work with someone she hates. Write a scene where she vents to her best friend. Include a moment where the best friend asks where these strong feelings are coming from: "I don't think you hate him . . ."

5. Write a scene where your protagonist finally separates from the person she's been forced to be with and then realizes how much she misses the other character.

Forbidden Love

Have you ever felt a desire you were told was wrong? Have you ever wanted someone who others said you couldn't have? Have you ever kept your love secret because you'd be ostracized if people knew what you did behind closed doors?

Forbidden Love is when two characters try to resist each other because society wouldn't approve—and then get together anyway. They won't let anyone tell them who they can love.

There are many reasons their love might be forbidden. They're married to other people. They come from different backgrounds and their parents don't approve. They have a power imbalance at work. They are distantly related. They're closely related, by marriage. (Unless you want to get *very* forbidden.) One of them is the other's teacher. Maybe one of them has a criminal record.

The taboo nature of their relationship is part of what makes it exciting. If anyone found out, there would be consequences. Depending on the kind of story you're telling, those consequences could be huge or relatively small, anything from disapproving gods destroying their planet to parents disowning them. But no matter what the end results might be, they are willing to risk it. Their love is that overpowering.

"You Can't Ever Tell Anyone about This"

◆ SCENARIO ◆

Because of their difference in social status, your protagonist and her lover don't see each other often. However, she receives a formal invitation to an important event, with a personal message from her lover: *Please come.* It's not safe for them to be seen together, but she goes anyway.

◆ BRAINSTORM ◆

What *are* the consequences of getting caught? Make sure you're clear on how bad things could get. The more specific, the better. When your protagonist arrives at this event, you want your readers to be thrilled—*she's there for her love*—and terrified—*she better not die for her love.*

◆ WRITE ◆

Write a scene where your protagonist and her forbidden lover are at a public event—a party, a coronation, an intergalactic town hall—and they must pretend they don't know each other. Build to a moment where they discreetly touch hands. A small moment, but intensely erotic.

◆ OPTIONAL ELEMENTS TO INCLUDE ◆

- The loosening of one button.
- A stifled gasp.
- A moment where they're standing so close to each other they can barely breathe.

Callbacks

How did these two characters meet? Let them find an excuse to talk about their initial connection. Make the subtext underneath everything they're saying: *I want you.*

"Meet Me in the Woods at Midnight"

◆ SCENARIO ◆

Your protagonist receives a message. Her lover wants to meet her at a time when she's supposed to be somewhere else. It's not like him to reach out like this. Too risky. So, it must be important. How can she go meet him without anyone finding out?

◆ BRAINSTORM ◆

What is your protagonist's home life like? Who does she live with? Who keeps tabs on her? Why is this person so controlling? Why do they feel like they can tell your protagonist what to do? Think about why your protagonist is afraid of them. What kind of punishments have they inflicted on your protagonist in the past? In what ways could they hurt her?

◆ WRITE ◆

Write a scene where your protagonist sneaks out. Think about everything she must do to get ready. What story does she have prepared if she gets caught? What is she feeling as she steps outside? Scared? Excited? Worried? What's it like outside—day or night, cold or hot, dry or wet? Has she taken any steps to make sure no one recognizes her? Use details to help your readers feel like they are escaping with your protagonist.

◆ OPTIONAL ELEMENTS TO INCLUDE ◆

- The sound of a door slamming.
- A broken heel.
- One of them arrives first—and for a moment, they think the other one won't come.
- A frantic kiss.

Fantasy Twist

What kind of magic exists in the world of your story? Can your protagonist perform any spells? What if she compels her loved ones to believe she's still home after she leaves? Is she powerful enough? And if so, does she get away with it? Or does the spell wear off before she gets back?

Callbacks

Think about what your protagonist wears when she sneaks out to meet her lover. Could it be something you've referenced earlier in your story? Maybe something she was wearing when she and her lover first met? An item of clothing that holds personal significance?

"I Want Every Part of You"

◆ SCENARIO ◆

Your protagonist and her forbidden lover finally have an entire evening to themselves. And a bed. The bed is important. This is the first time they've been able to lie down together. They are going to take advantage of this bed. Thank God for the bed!

◆ BRAINSTORM ◆

Write an interior monologue, from your protagonist's point of view, about everything she wants to do to, and with, her lover.

Write an interior monologue, from her lover's point of view, about everything he wants to do to, and with, your protagonist.

◆ WRITE ◆

Write a scene where your protagonist and her lover spend an entire night together for the first time. Have them take things slowly. They have all night, so there's no need to rush. They take advantage of their time by cataloging every part of each other's bodies.

Remember: They're still getting to know each other. Don't be afraid to let some of their encounter be awkward.

◆ OPTIONAL ELEMENTS TO INCLUDE ◆

- One of them is ticklish.
- A whispered request.
- Fingers running through hair.
- Rose petals on the bed.

Fantasy Twist

What if these two characters could pause time and spend an eternity together in one night? What would they do with all that time?

Quick Writes

Set a timer for 15 minutes and do not stop writing until the timer goes off. Do not edit, cross out, or censor yourself. Write down every thought that comes to you.

1. Write a scene where your protagonist hides under a bed to avoid being caught with her forbidden lover, and she ends up stuck there overnight.

2. Write a scene where your protagonist breaks up with her forbidden lover because she can't stand the lying and hiding. Have her be unnecessarily cruel—even though she doesn't mean it. She thinks if she's mean enough, maybe he'll actually stay away.

3. Write a scene where two supporting characters conspire to break up your protagonist and her forbidden lover.

4. Your protagonist's father disapproves of her relationship—but when he was younger, he was in a forbidden relationship of his own. Write a scene where your protagonist calls him out for his hypocrisy.

5. Write a scene where your protagonist announces her relationship to a huge crowd by kissing her lover in front of everyone. When someone tries to shame them, she makes an impassioned speech about why their love isn't wrong.

Second Chance Romance

$\mathscr{O}$nce upon a time, they were in love. Maybe they were high school sweethearts sneaking out at night to kiss in the moonlight. Maybe they dated in Sorcery Academy, but didn't need a love potion to fall head over heels. Maybe they even got married, but things didn't work out and they went their separate ways.

Lots of life has happened since then. They're worlds away from the people they used to be.

And yet. Sometimes they still think about each other. They wonder what the other one's up to. When something good happens, they want to tell each other. When one is going through a rough patch, they want to feel their former love's consoling embrace. They want, they need, they hope. But they were so young back then. What did they know? There's no use going back.

At least that's what they think—until their paths cross again and they discover the spark is still there. They feel alive in a way they haven't felt in ages. They decide to give this another go. They embark on a Second Chance Romance.

Will they finally get the Happily Ever After they missed out on before?

"I Can't Believe You Remember That"

◆ SCENARIO ◆

Your protagonist and her love interest haven't seen each other in years. They totally lost touch, so when they bump into each other today it's a shock. They're both dating other people. The smart thing to do would be to say hello and move on. But does anyone ever do the smart thing in situations like this?

◆ BRAINSTORM ◆

Come up with ten inside jokes they once shared, a few moments they each regret, and a silly memory they look back on fondly. What do they both miss about that time in their life? Perhaps there was a time when you told yourself, "Take a mental picture so you never forget this moment." Come up with a moment from their shared past when they both felt this way.

◆ WRITE ◆

Your protagonist bumps into her ex. This was the big ex, the one who got away. They both have other places to be, maybe they're even late. But instead of hurrying on, they sit down to talk and catch up. Write a scene where they unexpectedly rekindle the spark they once had for each other. They both know this could get complicated, but they let it happen anyway.

Remember: They weren't planning this meeting. They don't really have time for this. Keep the other parts of their lives alive during this scene to raise the stakes. By spending more time with their ex, they're making themselves late to something, making someone else wait for them, and potentially creating a problem for themselves that they will have to deal with later.

◆ OPTIONAL ELEMENTS TO INCLUDE ◆

- ♦ A hug that goes on a beat longer than most hugs.
- ♦ One of them is surprised to find themselves getting emotional.
- ♦ They decide to do this again.

Fantasy Twist

There are many ways people say "I love you" to each other without words. Can you think of any supernatural or fantastical ways they might show each other their love without "being bad" and saying the actual words?

"Maybe in Another Life"

◆ SCENARIO ◆

What if you could have another chance with a long-lost love or had unlimited do-overs until you got it right? Would you go for it? Even if your ex was no longer the same, or if all your loved ones told you to move on? But you miss them so deeply. You'd do anything to get them back.

◆ BRAINSTORM ◆

How might your protagonist be given an opportunity to reunite with a dead lover? Come up with a system and set of rules wherein this might be possible. In this world, is the science of "second chance romance" regulated? Is it safe?

◆ WRITE ◆

Write a scene where your protagonist goes through a series of interviews to determine if she is psychologically fit for second chance romance. The questions are invasive, but your protagonist is determined to convince everyone she is a good candidate.

Remember: Some second chances have ethical gray areas. Think about all the different ways this might go wrong.

◆ OPTIONAL ELEMENTS TO INCLUDE ◆

- False hope.
- A bribe.
- She needs a sample of her ex's DNA.

Fantasy Twist

Instead of making this a scientific process, what if your protagonist seeks out a witch or other spellcaster to make this second chance possible? They might warn her that these kinds of spells aren't always safe . . .

"Do You Think You Can Be Different This Time?"

◆ SCENARIO ◆

Your protagonist can't stop thinking about why things went wrong the last time she was with her newly rekindled flame. She wants assurances that they won't fall into the same patterns and make the same mistakes. He wants to know why they can't just move on without rehashing all that stuff.

◆ BRAINSTORM ◆

During their first attempt at romance, what recurring fights or issues did they have that they couldn't seem to move past? Write three quick versions of the same fight that used to be their core issue. Look at it from both of their perspectives.

◆ WRITE ◆

Write a scene where these characters try to heal an old wound. Your protagonist insists that if they really want to make it work this time, they need to do it right. Her love interest finally agrees. So, they talk, rationally and calmly, about their baggage. They know it may be difficult to navigate these potential land mines, but it's necessary for them to move forward.

Remember: Now that they have some distance from who they used to be, this conversation won't go the way it used to. They're older, and hopefully smarter. But that doesn't mean they're perfect. Find a moment in the scene where they become their former selves.

◆ OPTIONAL ELEMENTS TO INCLUDE ◆

- One of them calls the other one out for remembering something wrong.
- One of them expresses gratitude for the opportunity to try this again.
- One of them wants to leave before the other one feels the conversation is over.

Fantasy Twist

Does the world of your story have ways of seeing the past (other than photos and videos)? What if there was a way they could step back into their old selves and relive a moment, to see who's remembering it correctly? What if they could change a moment from the past that didn't go well?

Quick Writes

Set a timer for 15 minutes and do not stop writing until the timer goes off. Do not edit, cross out, or censor yourself. Write down every thought that comes to you.

1. Write a scene where your protagonist and her love interest revisit an important place from their past where they're haunted by ghosts of their previous relationship. Old wounds reopen.

2. Write a flashback scene showing the first time your protagonist and her love interest met. How are they different now, and how are they the same?

3. Your protagonist is afraid she will make the same mistakes she made last time. Write a scene where she expresses her fears to her best friend and asks for advice.

4. Write a scene where the newly recoupled pair visits his family. His mom confronts your protagonist by saying, "Don't break my kid's heart again."

5. Write a sex scene where your protagonist shows her rekindled love interest that she's learned a few things since the last time they were together.

Friends to Lovers

Here's how Friends to Lovers usually goes:
They have the kind of friendship people make movies about. Strong, dependable, trusting, playful. They're always there for each other. They put the best in best friends. But lately, they've been confused by what they're feeling. Let's just say, there are . . . stirrings of attraction.

Wait, no, stop. They can't do this. Their friendship is too good. Why potentially mess up this great thing for something that might not work?

But, oh God, if it *does* work??? Wouldn't it be everything they ever wanted? For their best friend and the love of their life to be the same person?

So they risk it.

WHAM, POW! The honeymoon stage is better than they imagined. It's a level of intimacy they didn't know was possible. *Oh, so you like that, eh? Oh, and you want* THAT*? Got it.*

Then they hit a roadblock. One of them breaks a promise (or a magical sacred pact, maybe?). It shouldn't hurt this bad because they knew this was a possibility. They knew what they could lose! But they let themselves be vulnerable. Now this betrayal feels like death.

Hopefully they can find their way back to each other. Because they worked as friends. And they worked even better as lovers. This relationship is worth fighting for—the stakes are high because neither can fathom losing the other.

"This Feels Impossible"

◆ SCENARIO ◆

Your protagonist and her best friend just had their first kiss. It wasn't planned. It just . . . happened. Now they're both confused. Where do they go from here?

◆ BRAINSTORM ◆

Make a list of reasons they think they shouldn't be together. Give them unique perspectives. Some of their reasons can overlap, but most of their reasons should be specific to how they each see the world.

◆ WRITE ◆

Write a scene where they have a rational discussion about why they shouldn't do this. Obviously, they won't stick to this decision. But for now, they're going to try.

Remember: They're kidding themselves when they say they don't want to be together. They might be saying "I think we should just be friends," but the subtext is "I want you so badly."

◆ OPTIONAL ELEMENTS TO INCLUDE ◆

- A signed contract.
- A favorite song.
- A canceled plan.

Fantasy Twist

What if your protagonist is given a glimpse of the future where she and her best friend aren't talking anymore? She doesn't know if it's just a possible future or if it's going to happen, but she doesn't want to tempt fate. This vision is what makes her hold back.

"Do That Thing You Always Do"

◆ SCENARIO ◆

Your protagonist knows her lover better than anyone. His likes and dislikes, hopes and dreams, and annoying habits. She knows he likes his coffee the color of almonds and his eggs runny. She knows he's 5'9" even though he says 5'10". Knowing each other so well has its advantages. But it also means they know how to hurt each other.

◆ BRAINSTORM ◆

Write a portrait of your protagonist. Include her likes, dislikes, habits (healthy and unhealthy), verbal tics, self-care routine, fears, needs, and wants. Do the same for her love interest. Does he have any words he overuses? What are his pet peeves? What are his biggest flaws? Your characters will use these details as ammunition.

◆ WRITE ◆

Write an emotionally bloody argument. Your protagonist is upset at her lover and feeling self-destructive. She's ready to throw a grenade on their relationship. She tells him to "do that thing you always do." In another context, this might be enticing, joyful. But now it cuts like a knife. Because she means something he does that she hates. "Do that thing you always do." Turn the word *always* into an accusation.

◆ OPTIONAL ELEMENTS TO INCLUDE ◆

- A mistake.
- One of your characters tries to leave, but the other one won't let them go.
- A gesture of kindness that is ignored.

Fantasy Twist

If your characters are nonhuman, think about the species-specific details they could use against each other in their fight. Don't feel like you have to stick to any lore you've read in other books. This world is your own creation, so you get to make the rules.

Callbacks

This scene takes place later in your story, after these friends have become lovers. Go back and read some of the earlier scenes you've written. Find a moment of happiness that they can bring up in this fight. But in their anger, they remember it differently. They warp a good memory and turn it into something that feels messy, ugly, wrong.

"I Promise I'll Never Hurt You"

◆ SCENARIO ◆

It's the morning after going from Friends to Lovers. The point of no return. They can't put love/lust back in the bottle! So, what do they do now? When your protagonist wakes up, she's confused. Not about last night. *That* was great. It's the "what comes next" that's scary.

◆ BRAINSTORM ◆

Think about your protagonist's past relationships. What lessons has she learned about love, and what does she still need to learn? Is she usually the breaker-upper or the one who gets broken up with? How have her breakups made her the person she is today?

Think about how her friend was there for her during these breakups. Was he the shoulder she cried on? Did he take her out for food to get her mind off her sadness? Examine their history.

◆ WRITE ◆

Write that morning-after scene. Your protagonist wakes up and tries to sneak out. Find the humor in this moment. How awkward and embarrassing can you make it? Before she gets out, her former-friend-now-lover catches her and asks where she's going. At first, she's afraid to tell him about her fears but he draws them out. Show your reader who he is and what he's made of. Give him a moment where he convinces your protagonist that what they did was right.

Remember: They know each other so well. She knows that when he makes a promise, he means it. So, the promise he makes to her in this scene should carry a lot of weight.

◆ OPTIONAL ELEMENTS TO INCLUDE ◆

- She compares him to one of her exes. He tells her why she's wrong.
- When sneaking out doesn't work, she tries to hide. Make a game out of it.
- Unexpected morning-after sex.

Fantasy Twist

When your protagonist gets caught trying to sneak out, she's so mortified she wants to disappear. What if she does disappear? What if her embarrassment is so powerful that it manifests itself in such a way that she literally blends into the background? But it's not that easy to get away from this guy. Because even when she disappears, he sees her. He really, really sees her.

Quick Writes

Set a timer for 15 minutes and do not stop writing until the timer goes off. Do not edit, cross out, or censor yourself. Write down every thought that comes to you.

1. How long has your protagonist known her friend-who-isn't-yet-her-lover? Write a scene where another friend points out the chemistry that's been obvious to others for years.

2. These friends aren't lovers yet. Write a scene where they're hanging out, it's late at night, maybe they're cuddling (but, you know, just as friends), and they talk about what they're both looking for in a partner. They're describing each other.

3. Your protagonist's friend is getting ready to move to another city, world, or galaxy. The prospect of losing him makes her realize what she really feels.

4. Write a sex scene where your protagonist and her lover can't stop laughing because how did they go from friends to *this*?!?

5. Write a scene where your protagonist expresses doubts about making this work, and her lover knows all the right things to say to calm her anxiety.

Fairy-Tale Retellings

*I*s your favorite fairy tale in the public domain? If you're not sure, google it now.

Are you back? Great. If it is in the public domain (meaning it's no longer under copyright and can be altered and used for other creative purposes), good news: You can make that story your own without worrying about getting sued! A Fairy-Tale Retelling is a modern twist on a classic story, which means the structure of your story has already been figured out for you. Your job is to come up with a version of this well-known story that feels uniquely *you*. How can you turn it on its head? What new perspective can you provide? What is your specific take on *Peter Pan*—can you breathe new life into the story by telling it through the eyes of a supporting character? How can you tell the story of "Beauty and the Beast" in a way that makes readers see it in a new light? If you could reinvent "Snow White," what changes would you incorporate to make it feel fresh in our current world?

Since you're writing romantasy, the best way to dig deeper into these familiar stories is through the love story. If you look at the original fairy tales, many of them only skim the surface when it comes to the romantic connections. Take this opportunity to go further.

"If You Eat That, You're Gonna Regret It"

◆ SCENARIO ◆

In *Alice in Wonderland*, Alice was presented with a cookie that had the words "Eat Me" written on it. The cookie made her grow bigger. Your protagonist faces a similar provocation. She has been given some kind of magical morsel that will change her. She doesn't know if the change will be good or bad. Most people wouldn't risk it. But your protagonist feels stuck. Maybe she isn't happy in her relationship, and she thinks her lover would like her better if she was different in some way. Regardless, she needs a change.

◆ BRAINSTORM ◆

What events led her to this moment of recklessness? What would it take for her to decide *not* to eat this food that could change her in a bad way? Why is she willing to take the risk?

◆ WRITE ◆

Your protagonist is walking home. It's late, dark, cold. A mysterious mentor character invites your protagonist into their home to rest. They offer something to eat, but with a warning: *This will change you.* Write a conversation where she debates how her lover might react to her changed and (hopefully) improved self, then impulsively goes for it.

Remember: There are endless ways you could write this scene. Perhaps she decides to take the food home to contemplate her decision further. She discusses it with her lover, who is against her eating it. Which ironically makes her want to eat it more.

◆ OPTIONAL ELEMENTS TO INCLUDE ◆

- A foul taste.
- A deep, calming breath.
- A moment of rejection.

Fantasy Twist

How extreme do you want to go with your protagonist's response to eating this magical food? In what ways might it transform her? What if it turns her into an entirely different person?

Callbacks

If you're writing your own version of *Alice in Wonderland*, list all the most important elements you want to include. In what ways can you make these callbacks to *Alice* recognizable but also uniquely your own?

"I Swear This Shoe Fit Yesterday"

◆ SCENARIO ◆

In "Cinderella," a glass slipper is the prince's only clue to finding his mystery woman. What if the shoe didn't fit? Would Cinderella try to convince the prince it was her? Or would she realize the prince is an idiot for not recognizing her voice and vibe, and she's probably better off without him? How might a shoe-that-doesn't-fit send her story in a completely different direction?

◆ BRAINSTORM ◆

It doesn't have to be a shoe your Cinderella stand-in leaves behind. In the movie *Another Cinderella Story*, Selena Gomez's modern-day Cinderella character, Mary Santiago, accidentally left her digital media player behind. (Inside Hollywood tidbit: In the script, which was cowritten by the author of this book, Mary left her iPod behind, but the studio got the rights to use a lesser-known media player, Zune, instead.) Make a list of identifying objects your protagonist might have with her that she could lose, then pick the one that feels most like your character.

◆ WRITE ◆

Write a scene where your protagonist accidentally leaves something behind at a ball or a party. Then write a scene where the guy she flirted with at the party uses this object to try to find her. Then do a hard left turn to make this Cinderella story your own, as your protagonist discovers this isn't the guy she wants to have her Happily Ever After with. Where do you go now?

Remember: You don't have to stick to the plot of the original "Cinderella," but it's helpful to use parallel plot points. They can be fun Easter eggs, and they give you a tried-and-tested structure to follow.

◆ OPTIONAL ELEMENTS TO INCLUDE ◆

- A fairy godmother surrogate character.
- An epiphany, wherein your protagonist lists all the reasons she needs to do her own thing.

Fantasy Twist

The original Cinderella didn't have any magical powers, but her fairy godmother did. What if your protagonist is her own fairy godmother? Think of the possibilities!

"I Don't Need You to Save Me"

◆ SCENARIO ◆

In many classic fairy tales, a princess is rescued by a prince. No thank you, patriarchy. She can save herself. For this prompt, take a classic heroine and give her more power. Flip the script so she doesn't need her love interest; he's more of a nice bonus.

◆ BRAINSTORM ◆

Look at the original version of the fairy tale you've chosen and make a list of moments when your heroine is active; then make a list of moments when she is passive. Think about how you can reimagine her story in a way that gives her more agency.

◆ WRITE ◆

Your protagonist faces great danger. A power-hungry royal, pirate, monster, witch, or stepmother wants her dead and threatens her love interest. Write a scene where she plans to save the day, even though no one believes in her. Write an impassioned speech where she convinces her allies to follow her. Show the moment where she grows into herself and becomes a leader.

◆ OPTIONAL ELEMENTS TO INCLUDE ◆

- A pact.
- A vision of utter destruction (in a reflective surface).
- A moment where she almost gives up but perseveres.

Fantasy Twist

Many favorite fairy tales include talking animals. Give your protagonist a furry friend who can help her succeed.

Quick Writes

Set a timer for 15 minutes and do not stop writing until the timer goes off. Do not edit, cross out, or censor yourself. Write down every thought that comes to you.

1. Write a scene where your protagonist kisses an object or a creature that then transforms into the love of her life.

2. Write a scene where a character with malicious intent disguises themselves as your protagonist and then seduces her lover.

3. Write a scene where your protagonist does something extreme to prove to a prince (or princess) that she's the one they're looking for.

4. Write a series of scenes where your protagonist makes a deal with a beastly character: *Set my loved one free and take me as your prisoner instead.*

5. Your protagonist suffers from a curse. Unless she finds true love soon, she will never [insert something she desperately wants]. But who is worthy of her?

Cozy Fantasy

*T*ime to put your feet up and relax—Cozy Fantasy means low stakes and lots of comfort. There aren't any big battles, medical emergencies, or family tragedies. Your protagonist's life won't ever be in danger. Nothing terrible happens. Readers turn to Cozy Fantasy to get away from the stress they find in so many other books.

Here are some of the things you will find in Cozy Fantasy stories: close-knit communities, solid friendships, good vibes, quaint cafés, inns, gardens, gossipy neighbors, flirtation, hunky barkeeps, magical creatures, light intrigue, mistaken identities, good coffee, little mysteries, scones, conversations by a fire, witty banter, and anything that makes you feel good.

Stories move at a slower pace in Cozy Fantasy. There's more emphasis on character than plot. But that doesn't mean there isn't drama. You can have drama without danger. Cozy isn't boring!

Just make sure the reader always feels safe and taken care of. They come to Cozy Fantasy for respite from the troubles of the real world—a balm for the soul.

Create the coziest world you can possibly imagine. Your readers will love you for it.

"Coffee or Tea?"

◆ SCENARIO ◆

Every day you make a thousand choices. You don't even notice most of the small ones. But what if you did? What if you paid attention to every little decision with a sense of gratitude? The fact that you get to make so many choices means you're alive, and that's a wonderful thing. That's the revelation your protagonist has just made and she's about to embrace it.

◆ BRAINSTORM ◆

Think through the last week. How many choices did you make without thinking about it? Try to make an exhaustive list. Can you even remember them all? Do this exercise to get a sense of all the choices your protagonist and her partner might make in their day-to-day lives.

◆ WRITE ◆

Your protagonist must make a difficult decision. It's not life or death, but it's big. Something like taking a promotion that would send her to another kingdom. Or having a child with her warlock husband. It could even seem superficial, like getting bangs, but it's a change she'll have to live with for a long time, so she can't treat it lightly.

Your protagonist feels frozen. So, instead of addressing the most pressing thing on her plate, she and her partner spend the day focusing on other decisions. See how long you can sustain this chain of choices until they come back to the one they've been avoiding.

Write their day of decisions.

◆ OPTIONAL ELEMENTS TO INCLUDE ◆

- A visit from a long-lost loved one who offers your protagonist helpful advice.
- A hesitant yes.
- A decisive no.
- A wary maybe.

Fantasy Twist

Not deciding can, in and of itself, be a decision. Is there anything supernatural your protagonist could do to put off the inevitable?

"Guess What I Made for You"

◆ SCENARIO ◆

Gifts are your protagonist's love language. She believes the best gifts are handmade. There's nothing like the feeling you get when someone cares enough to make a gift for you from scratch. It could be sewn, stitched, or drawn—when it's homemade, it comes from the heart, and those gifts mean so much more. Your protagonist and her lover are about to put this philosophy into action.

◆ BRAINSTORM ◆

What skills do your characters possess? Who's the better seamstress? The better builder? The better painter? Do some thinking about what kinds of things they might make for each other. Can you think of any gifts that would be especially nostalgic for each of them?

◆ WRITE ◆

Write a series of scenes where your protagonist and her partner make and give gifts to each other. Build momentum and create a sense of fun as they try to top each other with every gift. This is a great opportunity to have them show their love through actions rather than words: How can you express the ways in which these gifts are especially meaningful, based on how they craft for each other, the objects they make, and/or the materials they use?

◆ OPTIONAL ELEMENTS TO INCLUDE ◆

- A broken gift.
- A silly gift.
- A gift that's too big.
- A gift inside a gift.
- A misinterpreted gift.
- A gift that gets lost, then found, then lost again.
- A seasonal gift.

Fantasy Twist

Is it cheating to use magic to make something "by hand"? If your characters have powers, include a moment where one of them catches the other using magic and they tell them to stop. Gifts aren't as meaningful when you take shortcuts!

Callbacks

Create a gift that keeps giving. Interpret that however you want. Make it a gift your characters keep coming back to throughout the rest of your book. They aren't just making things; they're making memories. And every time you bring this object back into your story, it will remind your readers it was made with love. It can become a metaphor for the love your characters feel for each other.

"The Sexiest Thing You Could Do Is the Dishes"

◆ SCENARIO ◆

Dishes. Laundry. Taking out the trash. Many wouldn't consider chores sexy. But your protagonist loves a clean home. And her partner knows the way to her heart.

◆ BRAINSTORM ◆

Make a to-do list for your protagonist. Rank chores by order of importance. How much does each chore satisfy her? Which chores does she hate doing? Which ones does she enjoy because they calm the anxious voices in her head?

◆ WRITE ◆

Write a nontraditional foreplay scene. Think of something most people wouldn't consider erotic. It should be on your protagonist's to-do list. Her partner does it because he knows how relieved she'll be to not do it. The completion of this task *could* lead them to the bedroom . . . or back to the chore list.

Remember: Anticipation is sexy. How long can you make this pre-bedroom sequence of scenes last?

◆ OPTIONAL ELEMENTS TO INCLUDE ◆

- They run out of an important, specific cleaning product.
- The lover accidentally stains his clothes, leading to a striptease.

Fantasy Twist

What if your characters have a pet dragon, griffin, phoenix, or selkie? How would that complicate their daily routine? Do griffins need to be taken out for a walk? Are they always running out of dragon poop bags?

Quick Writes

Set a timer for 15 minutes and do not stop writing until the timer goes off. Do not edit, cross out, or censor yourself. Write down every thought that comes to you.

1. Write a scene where your protagonist and her love interest have a game night with friends. Show your reader how well they work together in a competitive situation.

2. Write a scene where your protagonist and her love interest get lost—but instead of freaking out about it, they turn their misadventure into the best day of their lives.

3. Your protagonist is a very old, anthropomorphized house. The only thing this old house cares about is keeping its inhabitants safe. Write a scene where the couple who lives there is put in danger by a storm, but the old house protects them.

4. Write a scene where a witchy protagonist gets home late and doesn't have time to prepare for a dinner party (or date), so she uses magic to clean, cook, and prep. The party is a wild success! Or maybe not. It might be more fun to show some magic gone awry.

5. Write a scene where two of your characters check in to an inn for the night, and they're so caught up in conversation they don't realize a battle is being waged outside.

Arranged Marriage

When a couple is forced to get engaged and possibly meet for the first time at their wedding, you've got the fascinating drama of an Arranged Marriage. This could happen for many reasons. It might be a traditional custom practiced by their parents, something your protagonist has been aware of (and perhaps dreading) for most of her life. Or an arrangement decided on by two warring groups to broker some sort of truce. An Arranged Marriage is often found in historical romance, and there are endless ways you could incorporate it into romantasy. In the world you create, this might even be the norm.

The relationship begins with distrust. Whatever these two characters expected, *this* isn't it. Your protagonist might feel like a visitor in her own home. She questions how she ended up here. What cruel joke is the universe playing on her?

But slowly things begin to change. As the characters get to know each other, a bond forms. Your protagonist is shocked that she's eagerly spending more time with this stranger. Seeing him doesn't feel like a chore anymore. And she's looking forward to their dinners together! She misses him when they're apart. And she's even curious about this stranger's touch. The thought of sharing a bed isn't as terrible as it once was. It's exciting. How did this happen?

When they finally develop true feelings for each other, they're taken aback. They should have seen this coming, but they're surprised every time.

"You're Not What I Expected... You're Better"

◆ SCENARIO ◆

Your protagonist had expectations for her Arranged Marriage. She envisioned what her spouse would look, sound, and smell like. She had ideas about what they would do with their lives, from their morning routine to what would happen in the bedroom. After they tied the knot, it was difficult for her to marry the fantasy with this flesh-and-bone, warts-and-all person. It turns out, real people are destined to be different from the fantasy version you've dreamt about!

◆ BRAINSTORM ◆

Write two detailed character descriptions of your protagonist's spouse, one titled "What I Thought My Spouse Would Be Like" and one titled "What My Spouse Is Really Like." Write both in your protagonist's voice. Be specific about how these two descriptions diverge.

Do the same exercise for the spouse, exploring their expectations of your protagonist. Give them different worldviews. In what ways do their beliefs, hopes, and dreams align with each other, and how are they opposed?

◆ WRITE ◆

It's the end of your book, after these characters fall in love. Your protagonist regrets her marriage ceremony. She felt like a guest at someone else's wedding. Her vows were impersonal. She tells her spouse she wants a do-over. Write a scene where her spouse improvises another, more meaningful, ceremony. This time, their vows come from the heart. Make these vows disarmingly personal, as they explicitly state how they've been fulfilled—and changed for the better—by each other's love.

◆ OPTIONAL ELEMENTS TO INCLUDE ◆

- A moment where your protagonist gets emotional and stumbles over her words.
- A moment where they hold hands to steady each other.
- A moment where one of them laughs, surprised by how well the other one knows them.

Callbacks

In what ways can this spontaneous ceremony mirror the earlier one, but with variation to show how their connection has deepened? Perhaps this could involve some magic that reveals your protagonist in a whole new light.

"Nope, Never, Not Now, Not Tomorrow, Not a Million Years from Now"

◆ SCENARIO ◆

What happens when you're in an Arranged Marriage and one of you tells the other "you'll change"? For anyone who has an independent spirit and doesn't trust this Arranged Marriage farce, these two little words are going to set off a bomb.

◆ BRAINSTORM ◆

Does your protagonist have a volatile temper? What usually sets her off? What does she look and sound like when she's mildly angry versus when her anger is off the charts? Does she have any coping mechanisms she uses to calm down? Perhaps some special powers?

◆ WRITE ◆

Your protagonist's spouse has embraced the Arranged Marriage. But your protagonist isn't there yet. Write a scene where her spouse is kind and says he can wait for her to come around, and then your protagonist delivers an epic diatribe explaining why she'll never change. Think of it as a rant of resistance, an aria of aversion. By the end of the scene, her spouse should regret ever implying your protagonist could love him.

Remember: "You'll change" might be the most infuriating words in the English language. They could be someone's villain origin story. They could create a rift between friends who never had conflict before. They could start a battle between peaceful nations. Give them the weight they deserve.

◆ OPTIONAL ELEMENTS TO INCLUDE ◆

- An object thrown across the room.
- A fear expressed.
- A long, uncomfortable moment where neither one of them will back down.

Callbacks

You know what's going to happen at the end of your story. The fact of the matter is your protagonist *will* eventually change her mind. Play around with the dramatic irony of this. What might she say in her speech now that you can refer to later with some humor?

"Why Does It Feel Like We've Known Each Other Forever?"

◆ SCENARIO ◆

Time goes so fast when you're having fun. But what if you suddenly find yourself married to someone you're afraid to open up to? What if you can barely talk to them because you don't want to get hurt? What if you refuse to engage in your own life because you didn't want this marriage in the first place? Suddenly time doesn't feel strange; it feels like a prison. But the miraculous thing about time is that it can change too.

◆ BRAINSTORM ◆

Why might your protagonist resist the idea that an Arranged Marriage could ever work? Do a deep dive into her former life and examine her previous romantic relationships, familial relationships, and friendships. Find one or two events from her past where she learned not to trust people.

◆ WRITE ◆

Write a scene where your protagonist finally opens herself up and embraces her new life. Pick an event or experience that triggers this growth. Take her from being resistant to being all in. It should feel like a key unlocking a door. The floodgates have opened.

Remember: You could know someone your whole life but never really know them. Then there are other people you click with so quickly and fully that hours feel like seconds when you're together. You know you have something special when you find yourself wondering, *How can this relationship still be so new when it feels like we've been together forever?* What does it take for your protagonist to finally feel this way?

◆ OPTIONAL ELEMENTS TO INCLUDE ◆

- She cooks something for her spouse.
- She fixes something her spouse accidentally broke.
- She makes a detailed plan for their joint future.

Fantasy Twist

What if these two characters met in another life? Maybe even in a life before that one, and another life before that. What if they keep doing this again and again, and every time their souls find each other again it feels like a miracle?

Callbacks

What was your protagonist's first impression of her spouse? Have her bring that up in this scene. Play around with the idea that they already felt like they knew each other, but your protagonist wasn't yet ready to admit it back then.

Quick Writes

Set a timer for 15 minutes and do not stop writing until the timer goes off. Do not edit, cross out, or censor yourself. Write down every thought that comes to you.

1. Write a scene where your protagonist and her love interest see each other for the first time and realize they've met before. How does their previous interaction influence their feelings about their upcoming nuptials?

2. Write a scene where your protagonist sneaks out of the house on her wedding night. What does her spouse do to convince her to come back?

3. Write a scene where your protagonist decides to share a bed with her spouse for the first time. Is she ready to go all the way?

4. Write a scene where your married protagonists discover they have more in common than they realized. The more mutual interests they discover, the giddier they get. Is this what true love feels like?

5. Write a scene where one of your married protagonists learns that their spouse chose them for the Arranged Marriage. This betrayal feels like a punch in the gut. Or could this be a good thing?

Slow Burn

*I*f you want to tease out the romance in your story to heighten the suspense, write a Slow Burn. Make your readers wait. For. Them. To. Get. Together. Make them start to wonder *if* it's going to happen or not. Make them ache for the first touch, the first kiss, and all the rest that comes with romance.

Slow Burn doesn't mean their connection is weak or fragile. Just the opposite. Show your readers every step from that first spark of mutual attraction through the process of getting to know each other and falling in love. Build their connection brick by brick. By the time it gets physical, your readers should be in a state of anticipation so intense they're ready to explode.

There's no formula to the Slow Burn. Some might say it means your characters get together at the halfway point; others will argue it shouldn't happen until the last chapter. If your characters take their time to get to know each other, it's a Slow Burn; if consummation happens early in your romantasy, that's a Fast Burn; and if it happens near the midpoint, that's a Normal Burn. When you're writing, take this advice to heart: The slower your burn, the more readers yearn.

"Wait, Not Yet, No, No, Okay Now"

◆ SCENARIO ◆

Your main characters have been Slow Burning for a while now. The anticipation is palpable. They're finally ready to get it on. *Tonight*. But instead of mauling each other like animals, they're taking *this* slow too.

◆ BRAINSTORM ◆

Think about the couple at the center of your story. What are their turn-ons? Map out their bodies with words. Think about how erotic they can be with each other before they remove their clothes.

◆ WRITE ◆

Write the slowest sex scene ever. Make the slowness a feature, not a bug. These two characters want to take their time. They waited so long for this moment that they deserve to really savor it. It's their reward for incredible patience.

◆ OPTIONAL ELEMENTS TO INCLUDE ◆

- The removal of one item of clothing at a time.
- Gentleness.
- Soft skin.
- A moment of quickening.

Fantasy Twist

What if one of these characters is supernatural and the other is human? How might that add a greater sense of discovery as they explore each other's physical forms for the first time?

"One Day You're Going to Love Me"

◆ SCENARIO ◆

Your protagonist is a hopeful romantic. The person she loves isn't available—maybe he's married, or he lives in another galaxy, or he's prioritizing his studies at a spellcaster academy over relationships. Whatever the reason, your protagonist knows she can't be with this person right now. But she has faith that it'll happen someday. She can wait.

◆ BRAINSTORM ◆

What does your protagonist love about this person? Be specific. Come up with ten moments they've shared over the years that made her think, *One day we'll be together*. This shouldn't be a one-sided love, so examine how he shows his love too, even without making a commitment.

◆ WRITE ◆

Your protagonist decides to write a letter to him. But instead of sending it, she keeps it. One day, when they get together, your protagonist will give this letter to the love of her life. The act of writing it and holding on to it is a way of saying, "I always knew this was going to happen." Write that letter now and make it disgustingly gushy and gooey—romantic beyond all reason.

Remember: Just because she writes this letter doesn't mean her love interest will ever read it. Where does she keep the letter? How might she react if the letter got lost, destroyed, or stolen before she had a chance to give it to him? Does she have a magical power that enables her to re-create the letter in an instant?

◆ OPTIONAL ELEMENTS TO INCLUDE ◆

- "The first time I knew . . ."
- "I almost told you when . . ."
- "Did you ever notice . . ."

Callbacks

The longer the Slow Burn goes on, the more special moments you can have your protagonist reference in her letter. Pick three events for your protagonist to describe in great detail.

"The Wait Was Worth It"

◆ SCENARIO ◆

These two characters have been through so much together. They've celebrated each other's successes and cried on each other's shoulders. The world is always changing—they've lost friends, lovers, family members. But they have one constant: each other.

◆ BRAINSTORM ◆

Are these characters good at waiting? Think about the moment right before the scene you're about to write. What is their emotional headspace? Maybe they're afraid to take the next step—or so excited to finally move forward that they can't think about anything else.

◆ WRITE ◆

Write a scene where your main characters consummate their relationship—and they go feral. Since they met, the pressure's been building and suddenly the dam has burst—once they start, they can't stop. Think of this as the opposite of a "fade to black" scenario—be explicit. Flex your erotic writing muscles. Get so graphic that you embarrass yourself. They have a lot of lost time to make up for.

◆ OPTIONAL ELEMENTS TO INCLUDE ◆

- They take a snack and water break.
- Their lovemaking travels from one location to another.
- Torn clothes.

Fantasy Twist

Consider how bodies differ in the fantasy world of your story. Does your protagonist have any unique and unusual erogenous zones?

Quick Writes

Set a timer for 15 minutes and do not stop writing until the timer goes off. Do not edit, cross out, or censor yourself. Write down every thought that comes to you.

1. Write a scene where your two main characters exchange either shoulder or foot massages, but they don't go further. These small moments of touch are almost too intense.

2. Your protagonist is surprised to discover she's attracted to a coworker she's known forever. Write a scene where she confides in her best friend. Where did these feelings come from? Have they always been there?

3. Your protagonist and her love interest are all about the "emotional slow burn": They can get physical as long as they keep their emotions separate. Write a scene where they talk through the rules of their situationship, but here's the subtext: They're starting to develop feelings, but neither one wants to admit it.

4. Write a scene where your protagonist introduces her (future) love interest to her parents. The way he treats them makes her see him in a new light.

5. Write an almost-kiss scene between your protagonist and a character who is growing on her. It's okay if you want to take it further—as long as you make it the slowest kiss in history.

LOVE TRIANGLE

*C*haracters tangled up in a Love Triangle are always compelling. Well, almost always. The problem that plagues badly written Love Triangles is when one of the potential lovers is *clearly* the wrong choice. Readers are stuck waiting for the protagonist to figure out something they've known all along. They want to scream at their book, "Why don't you see what I see???"

So, here's the key to a good Love Triangle: Make them *both* the right choice. Suddenly the audience is intrigued. Their allegiances shift back and forth as they root for one coupling, then the other. They don't want anyone to be heartbroken. Yet someone is bound to get crushed. The stakes are high.

If your protagonist chooses Lover A, her life will go in one direction. If she chooses Lover B, her life will look completely different. Both potential lives could be wonderful though! That's what gets your readers invested: They don't know which wonderful life to root for.

These stories have built-in suspense. The triangle itself makes the outcome more of a mystery. Your job is to let the plot thicken as the emotions of your lovers fluctuate from joy and love to jealousy and hate and back again. There's no easy solution in this scenario. That's what makes Love Triangles so juicy.

"I'll Tell Her What You Told Me to Say If She Tells You"

◆ SCENARIO ◆

When you're torn between two potential love interests, your communication skills are put to the test. What did you say to whom? It gets even more complicated when your love interests know about each other, and everything's a competition.

◆ BRAINSTORM ◆

How different are the love interests? Write a character profile for each. Some questions: How do they resolve conflict? What are they insecure about? Why do they like your protagonist? Who's more intimately compatible with the protagonist? What are their attachment styles, strengths, and weaknesses?

◆ WRITE ◆

Write a scene where the love interests compare notes, trying to figure out who's the favorite. The scene becomes an interrogation, then a competition to prove whose relationship is superior. They each eventually agree to disappear if she confirms she loves the other one more. But they can't control what she does, so nothing goes as planned.

◆ OPTIONAL ELEMENTS TO INCLUDE ◆

- The conversation almost comes to blows.
- A moment of sympathy.
- The destruction of private property.

Callbacks

When the love interests compare notes about their respective relationships with your protagonist, they should reference earlier scenes. Use dramatic irony by having them each say things that your reader knows are false, but which the other love interest believes to be true.

"This Wasn't Meant for Me, Was It?"

◆ SCENARIO ◆

Your protagonist sees something at the store that reminds her of one of her (two) lovers. It's a little thing, but it's meaningful. She purchases it on a whim. But then—oh no—she accidentally gives it to the wrong love interest.

◆ BRAINSTORM ◆

What's the perfect gift your protagonist might buy for her love interest? Make it unique and maybe a little unusual. If it's too generic, the wrong love interest wouldn't have any reason to suspect this gift isn't for him. It should be an obvious mistake if the wrong person opens it.

◆ WRITE ◆

Write the scene where your protagonist buys the gift, write the scene where she gives it to the wrong love interest, and then write the fallout of her mistake. Is your protagonist able to talk her way out of this?

◆ OPTIONAL ELEMENTS TO INCLUDE ◆

- A price tag.
- Doubling down on a lie.
- An abrupt departure.

Fantasy Twist

Close your eyes and visualize the location where she finds the gift. What makes it unique to the world of your story? Quickly jot down some visual details you might use.

"You Have to Make a Choice"

◆ SCENARIO ◆

Most Love Triangles end with a decision being made. (Unless you're writing a "why choose" story, where your protagonist ultimately decides two lovers are better than one.) Your protagonist has been agonizing over this decision. She isn't ready to make it. She wants more time. But time's taken away from her when she's confronted with an ultimatum.

◆ BRAINSTORM ◆

Which love interest would be most likely to give your protagonist an ultimatum? Do you think an ultimatum might work, or is it more likely to push your protagonist away?

Imagine two different scenarios. How might your protagonist react if Lover A gives her an ultimatum versus Lover B? What does each scene look like? Which scene has more tension? Which is more suspenseful? Which scene do you think your readers would find more satisfying?

◆ WRITE ◆

Pick the version of the ultimatum that you think has more energy and write that scene. Your protagonist does not see the ultimatum coming. She was looking forward to a fun night, when suddenly the rug is pulled out from under her. If you want to make the scene more compelling, set it up so she must make her choice in front of both love interests.

Remember: Just like choosing both is an option, so is choosing neither. Your protagonist might not like being put in such an awkward position. She might decide that anyone who would make her choose isn't the one for her. She might end up choosing . . . herself.

◆ OPTIONAL ELEMENTS TO INCLUDE ◆

- ◆ An unfair comparison.
- ◆ A fistful of cash.
- ◆ A moment that goes on longer than it should.

Fantasy Twist

You might create suspense by having the outside world encroach on this scene. An emergency distracts the love interests before your protagonist gives her answer.

Callbacks

Someone's about to get the short end of the "pick me" stick. His heart will be broken. Your protagonist might try to let him down gently, reminding him of good times from earlier in your story by saying something like, "We'll always have [insert event from an earlier chapter]."

Quick Writes

Set a timer for 15 minutes and do not stop writing until the timer goes off. Do not edit, cross out, or censor yourself. Write down every thought that comes to you.

1. Write a scene where your protagonist accidentally schedules two dates with two suitors on the same night. She tries to go on both dates without them finding out. Maybe she has the power to conjure up a second self to help her out.

2. Alternately, write a scene where your protagonist schedules two dates on the same night, and she's upfront about it. She tells them the truth and makes it a dinner for three.

3. Write a scene where your protagonist has a threesome with both of her suitors. Midway through, one of them chickens out and discreetly exits.

4. Alternately, write a threesome scene where both of your protagonist's suitors are game. How does this change the dynamics of their Love Triangle?

5. Write a scene where one of your protagonist's suitors gives her scandalous information about her other guy. Lover B claims it's a lie. Which one of them is telling the truth?

Healthy Relationships

*E*ven characters in Healthy Relationships don't live in a perfect world.

They're probably in therapy, right? They have fights, misunderstandings, bad days. But they know how to work through their differences with care and grace. They remember birthdays and anniversaries. They do things they know the other one wants or needs without being asked. They love talking to each other. They're playful and spontaneous in the bedroom, or the living room, or the backyard, or the jacuzzi, or the woods, or wherever they decide they want to be intimate.

They always put the other one first. They support each other. They are kind. They are the couple every other couple wants to be.

However, just because they're in a Healthy Relationship doesn't mean their stories lack conflict or drama. There can be plenty of that. But when disaster strikes, they face it together. They depend on each other. They know how to communicate nuance to each other without words. And when it comes to words, it's like they have their own special language—they have codes and signs and phrases that no one else understands. They will risk their lives for each other.

Send them to hell and back. At the end of your romantasy, their bond will be stronger than ever.

"Can We Talk about This?"

◆ SCENARIO ◆

Chaos is everywhere. It could be dragons ravaging your protagonist's small town, or Zeus and Poseidon engaging in an epic battle with no concern for the human victims, or highlanders pillaging your characters' village. Whatever it is, it's big. In the center of this high-stakes action, your protagonists have marital strife to work through. All while trying to get to safety.

◆ BRAINSTORM ◆

The couple at the heart of your story has a strong, healthy marriage (or long-term relationship). But let's get to the exciting part. What are the five biggest fights they've ever had and how did they resolve them?

◆ WRITE ◆

Your protagonist and her spouse are awakened in the middle of the night by trouble outside. They must evacuate and get to higher ground for safety. But as they prepare to leave, one of them does something that upsets the other. Maybe it stirs up a bigger issue they need to deal with. Write this scene and the ensuing fight.

Have them work through every stage of their argument while dealing with the danger outside. Find comedy in the contrast between what's going on around them and their ability to stay focused on their marital issue, which is way more pressing than this other nonsense. The war around them is just noise. By the time they reach the end of their journey, they resolve their fight. They've gotten to the root of their issues, and they feel better. End it all with a kiss.

◆ OPTIONAL ELEMENTS TO INCLUDE ◆

- They hide in the wreckage of a building, while calmly talking through their fight.
- They run from attackers, while calmly talking through their fight.
- They pause briefly during an explosion, then continue calmly talking through their fight.

Fantasy Twist

This is a great opportunity for some fun worldbuilding. What new parts of their world and environment can you introduce to your readers while your characters make their way to safety?

"I Have a Surprise for You"

◆ SCENARIO ◆

It's the main couple's anniversary. Your protagonist's partner has teased to her that he has a big surprise waiting. But then a worldly disaster (of your choice) strikes, and they are swept into battle. They work together to fight the monster, save the castle, defeat the demons. But the main thing on your protagonist's mind the whole time is: *Will I get home in time for my surprise?!*

◆ BRAINSTORM ◆

What is your protagonist's love language? This might help you determine what kind of surprise her partner would get for her. Is it a physical gift or an activity? Either way, you're going to create a lot of suspense, so make sure it's good. Come up with ten possibilities and try to top yourself with each one. When you think you know what it should be, go bigger.

◆ WRITE ◆

For this prompt, you're going to write three scenes. Write the scene where your protagonist's spouse teases the surprise he has waiting. Then, write a scene where it looks like she won't survive long enough to get back home for the surprise. Finally, write a scene where the surprise is revealed. A beginning, a middle, and an end. Think about what markers along this journey will make the arc of this day the most satisfying for your readers.

◆ OPTIONAL ELEMENTS TO INCLUDE ◆

- An empty box.
- Someone disappears into a portal.
- Your couple gets trapped in a small space. Will they ever get home?

Fantasy Twist

Your readers will assume your protagonist will eventually find out what her surprise is, so how can you subvert those expectations? What if your protagonist or her spouse dies (before being brought back to life)? Use the fantastical world of your story to toy with your readers' emotions and make them want to know what the surprise is as much as your protagonist does.

"This Is All I've Ever Wanted"

◆ SCENARIO ◆

Your protagonist knows a secret about her love interest. A secret her love is keeping about his identity. It could be a power he has, a world he's from, or a species he belongs to. Make it something he's been mocked or ridiculed for by small-minded people. Your protagonist wants him to feel safe enough to let her in. But she gets why he's hesitant. These are scary times. Your protagonist can wait until he's ready.

◆ BRAINSTORM ◆

Think about the prejudices and biases people in the world of your story hold. How have people been persecuted for being like your protagonist's love interest?

◆ WRITE ◆

Write the scene where the love interest opens up to your protagonist. Let your readers into his head. Make his fears palpable. But your protagonist says the right things. She doesn't make her lover feel shame. Her love is unconditional.

◆ OPTIONAL ELEMENTS TO INCLUDE ◆

- A frantic and fun makeout session.
- A compliment.
- A moment where they both feel giddy.

Callbacks

How long has your protagonist known her lover's truth? She might bring up a moment from their shared past, explaining how and when she put two and two together. Make it clear that she never wanted to put any pressure on her lover.

Quick Writes

Set a timer for 15 minutes and do not stop writing until the timer goes off. Do not edit, cross out, or censor yourself. Write down every thought that comes to you.

1. Your protagonist and her lover are getting intimate. Write a tender scene where they pause to check in and reestablish consent. Make each "Is this still okay?" sexy and fun.

2. Your protagonist brings home a dragon or other mythical creature and asks her partner if they can keep it. They have a delightful time with their new pet, but it's clear their "parenting" skills will be tested.

3. Your protagonist has had a long, hard day. Write a scene where her lover listens to her vent about every little annoyance, then makes her feel heard and seen.

4. Write a scene where your protagonist and her partner daydream about a big adventure they want to go on. End the scene when a decision is made. They're doing this.

5. Write a scene where your protagonist and her spouse have a near-death experience that leads to a recommitment ceremony to celebrate that they're still alive and together.

Mutual Pining

What could be worse than unrequited love? What if you thought your love was unrequited, but you had it all wrong?

Blame it on the secrecy, self-deception, and misunderstandings inherent in Mutual Pining.

Your protagonist is certain the object of her affection either doesn't know she exists or doesn't feel the same way. She tries to bury her feelings. But it's no use. She aches with yearning. Her emotions are intense. She's convinced she will never find happiness because she'll never have a Happily Ever After with her one and only true love.

Ironically, she couldn't be more wrong: Her crush loves her back! And her crush is equally tortured. *There's no way she could ever love me back*, he thinks. *My love is hopeless!*

This is your basic Mutual Pining setup. To pine is to yearn deeply, helplessly, desperately. And boy do these characters pine.

The trick with Mutual Pining is creating a scenario where your characters don't seem like idiots for not knowing the other one's true feelings. If their feelings are obvious but they're just afraid to act on them, that's more Mutual Timidity than Mutual Pining. Create obstacles and situations that make it harder for them to realize their feelings are mutual.

"They Don't Know I Exist"

◆ SCENARIO ◆

Your two main characters haven't met. But they're obsessed with each other. Come up with a scenario where their lives intersect but they don't have many opportunities to talk. Such as:

- They live in neighboring buildings and can see into each other's homes.
- They're public figures and they keep running into each other at media appearances.
- They have the same therapist but only meet as they arrive and depart their sessions.
- They're both in the same starship battalion but one of them outranks the other, and you're not allowed to fraternize outside your rank.

They have seen each other so often that they've both begun to create stories about each other.

◆ BRAINSTORM ◆

What might they both be able to learn about each other from outside sources? Do they have mutual friends? Imagine they've been asking around and trying to dig up as much (juicy, fun) dirt on the other person as possible. If they each assembled a dossier on the other one, what details would they be able to gather? Get personal.

◆ WRITE ◆

Write two parallel scenes that show your readers how similar these two characters are and therefore how right they are for each other. In each scene, have them talk to their respective best friends about what they've learned about their crush. Have them echo each other at least three times—an echo would be a moment where they say the exact same thing.

◆ OPTIONAL ELEMENTS TO INCLUDE ◆

- A physical trait they both share.
- Two separate moments where they each worry about being creepy.
- Two separate moments where they each express how they feel incomplete.

Fantasy Twist

If your characters aren't human, think about alternative ways they might snoop on each other (without being creepy about it). Is there a version of your story where they might be able to hear each other's thoughts? How would that change the dynamics of their relationship?

"I Feel Like I Might Explode"

◆ SCENARIO ◆

Your protagonist has been holding her feelings in for so long she's worried she might explode. But she isn't sure how her crush feels, and she doesn't want to mess up their friendship if her feelings are unrequited. Another friend suggests she hook up with someone else to defuse her sexual longings. This friend suggests she pretend this other person is her crush, maybe even throw in a little role-play. Maybe it'll help her work this crush out of her system?

◆ BRAINSTORM ◆

Let's say role-playing doesn't come naturally to your protagonist. Brainstorm all the ways she might be bad at this. Find the comedy in her horny awkwardness. Make a list of all the embarrassing and funny things she could do wrong.

◆ WRITE ◆

Write a sexy-but-silly scene where your protagonist hooks up with the wrong person. Everything about this encounter feels off. This isn't the person she wants to be with, so she tries to imagine it's her crush, but that only makes it worse. Think of this as train wreck sex. Your readers won't be able to turn away, even though they might be dying inside because of what an awful time your protagonist is having.

Remember: Your protagonist isn't into the surrogate sex she's having with the-one-who-is-not-her-crush, but it's still consensual and she's in charge. She's here because she thinks it will tamp down her unanswered longing. She's wrong.

◆ OPTIONAL ELEMENTS TO INCLUDE ◆

- Your protagonist puts her foot in her mouth. (Metaphorically or literally—you decide.)
- Limbs getting too tangled up in each other.
- A weird rhythm.

Fantasy Twist

Your protagonist is a witch or at least has access to potions. What if she tries an anti-horniness potion and she's dismayed to find that it doesn't work?

"Do You Think He Saw Me Staring at Him?"

◆ SCENARIO ◆

Pining comes with insecurity. There's doubt and second-guessing. And the most agonizing thing of all: Every interaction you have with the object of your affection gets dissected endlessly.

Your protagonist has a crush she's been obsessed with. Her friends feel like they've given the same answers to your protagonist's "what if" questions at least a million times. But all that's about to change because your protagonist is going to find out how her crush feels about her, in a completely unhealthy way.

◆ BRAINSTORM ◆

What does the crush think about lying? Does he have a rigid moral compass? Now remember, this is a Mutual Pining situation, so he's equally obsessed with your protagonist—but how deep does his obsession go? If he found out your protagonist did something shady, would it change how he feels? Brainstorm ten red flags he would consider relationship deal-breakers.

◆ WRITE ◆

Write a scene where your protagonist eavesdrops on her crush to find out what he thinks of her. She's tired of pining—she needs answers! You decide what her method of eavesdropping entails. Does she go old school and just listen through a door? Does she go tech savvy and bug one of her crush's devices? Or does she go supernatural and use a spell or telepathy? Whatever she does, she should learn a lot. Not just her crush's romantic inclinations, but something personal that her crush absolutely would *not* want her to know. Knowing this thing makes everything messy.

◆ OPTIONAL ELEMENTS TO INCLUDE ◆

- Stumbling.
- A startling confession.
- A moment of fear.

Callbacks

When your protagonist overhears her crush talking about her, he might reference a specific thing your protagonist said, or how hot she looked in a certain outfit.

Quick Writes

Set a timer for 15 minutes and do not stop writing until the timer goes off. Do not edit, cross out, or censor yourself. Write down every thought that comes to you.

1. Your protagonist is an immigrant in a new world. She's fallen in love with an intergalactic customs officer. It's love at first sight for both. Write a scene where she *almost* professes her love but stops for fear of being arrested.

2. Write a scene where your protagonist gets drunk (on alcohol or a spirit specific to the world you've created) and confesses her love . . . to the wrong person.

3. Write a scene where your protagonist decides she's going to come clean about her feelings, but her best friend convinces her not to.

4. Write a scene where your protagonist overhears the object of her affections talking about being in love—he's talking about her, but she misinterprets it.

5. Write a scene where the crush leaves a love note for your protagonist, but the note is either misplaced or destroyed before she finds it.

Only One Bed

The Only One Bed trope is a cousin of Forced Proximity. Here's the difference: While not all romantic relationships have Forced Proximity built into them, every romantic couple could face the possibility of Only One Bed. Also, Forced Proximity situations take place over long periods, whereas Only One Bed scenarios last for just one night. Oh, but it's the most agonizing and tantalizing night ever. Cue the tension!

There are many different situations where your protagonist and her love interest could find themselves faced with this dilemma. They're traveling together for work and stop at a small hotel for the night, but there's only one available room. They're camping and one of their packs got left behind, which means they only have one tent . . . and only one sleeping bag. They're on their way to another galaxy and one of the sleep pods accidentally got ejected, which means two people must share one pod. Be creative. The best Only One Bed situation is one that comes as a surprise—to both your characters and your readers.

This trope can be as spicy as you like. If your story is high on the smut scale, this is a great opportunity to take your characters there for the first time. But if they aren't ready to progress that far in their relationship, you can use Only One Bed to ratchet up the anticipation. When it comes to sex in romantasy, the journey is as important as the destination.

" Close Your Eyes "

◆ SCENARIO ◆

Your protagonist and her rival/boss/friend are handcuffed to each other during a prank or game set up by friends or coworkers. But here's the catch: The key is inaccessible until the next day. Though there are plenty of beds they *could* sleep in tonight, it isn't physically possible for them to separate.

◆ BRAINSTORM ◆

Think about how complicated this could get. Changing into pajamas, brushing your teeth, and blowing your nose are suddenly difficult. And then there's bathing. How many awkward situations can you create before bed? And then what? Think about where each body part lands as two people who can't get away from each other try to maintain some distance.

◆ WRITE ◆

Write this scene where they're cuffed together, starting with the click of the lock and going until they get the key. They should each have their own arc throughout this escapade. In what ways do they grow together?

◆ OPTIONAL ELEMENTS TO INCLUDE ◆

- A moment where one of them has to pee.
- An aborted attempt at changing clothes.
- An unexpected moment of calm.

Callbacks

As they're trying to fall asleep, have them talk about their first impressions of each other. One of them realizes, "I made an assumption about you, but I was wrong."

"How Did We Get Here?"

◆ SCENARIO ◆

Your two main characters don't like each other, but they also don't really know each other very well. And suddenly, due to circumstances outside their control—but in yours—they find themselves sharing a bed. *Now* what? They aren't going to get physical; that's not where they are in their relationship. But they have to do *something*. They can't just lie here and not acknowledge each other. Which is why they start talking. And they have a conversation that surprises them both.

◆ BRAINSTORM ◆

Your first impression of a person isn't always right. Put yourself in both characters' heads and do some freewriting about what they think about each other. Figure out all the preconceived ideas they've perhaps incorrectly formed.

◆ WRITE ◆

Write a scene where your protagonist and her potential love interest have their first real conversation. They just happen to be sharing a bed. The intimacy of their situation causes them to talk in ways they wouldn't otherwise and say things they never thought they'd tell this person.

When they start talking, it might be awkward. They are slow to connect. But after they talk for a while, the floodgates open. They both go deeper than they're used to going, and they open up about things that would take most new couples five or six dates to get to. This conversation will change their relationship.

◆ OPTIONAL ELEMENTS TO INCLUDE ◆

- Their feet touch.
- One of them makes an embarrassing confession.
- A difficult question.
- A promise that's going to be tough for them to keep.

Callbacks

"I can't believe I thought you [insert misconception here]." This is a chance for these characters to be completely honest with each other and move forward in their relationship, transformed. You might have one of them talk about the first time they met and what they got wrong.

"You Stay on Your Side, I'll Stay on Mine"

◆ SCENARIO ◆

Your protagonist is stuck sharing a room with Her Worst Enemy. Her skin crawls at the sight of him. His voice makes her nauseous. The thought of sharing a bed makes her want to scream. But here they are, in this dumb predicament. She's upset about the entire situation, but she's not just going to lie down and pretend she's okay with him. Absolutely not. She will make sure he knows she doesn't want to be here. She will do her best to make it feel like they're both alone.

◆ BRAINSTORM ◆

Why does she detest this guy? Map out the arc of their relationship leading up to this moment. Start with their first meeting and come up with a handful of relationship markers—moments when her feelings intensified. Figure out why her indifference turned to dislike and then hatred. And what about him? What is he thinking about all of this? Are his feelings the same as hers?

◆ WRITE ◆

Write a scene where your protagonist makes it clear that, even though she might be sharing a bed with this guy, they will not, under any conditions, make physical contact. You might have her start by building a wall of pillows on the bed to establish boundaries: "You get that side, I get this side, and don't you dare move a pillow." Don't stop there. How else can she touch-proof her side of the bed?

◆ OPTIONAL ELEMENTS TO INCLUDE ◆

- Tussling over the sheets.
- A moment where her hand or foot accidentally crosses the pillow border.
- A moment where he surprises her.

Fantasy Twist

Does your protagonist have access to magic? If she could put a protective spell on either herself or on her side of the bed, what would she do?

Quick Writes

Set a timer for 15 minutes and do not stop writing until the timer goes off. Do not edit, cross out, or censor yourself. Write down every thought that comes to you.

1. Write a scene where your protagonist and her biggest rival seek shelter in a bunker during a disaster, but there's Only One Bed.

2. Write a scene where your protagonist and her (mutually pining) best friend crash their vehicle in the middle of nowhere. They try to walk back to civilization, but it's getting dark. If they want to survive the night without freezing, they'll have to cuddle.

3. Write a scene where your protagonist is with a group of four friends at an inn with only three beds. They play a game to determine who gets the couch. Your protagonist loses. But in the middle of the night, one of her friends invites her into his bed.

4. A natural disaster has trapped your protagonist and her best friend in a vehicle. There's room to sleep in the back . . . but it'll be tight.

5. Your protagonist isn't human. She's stuck sharing a bedroom with her crush, who she doesn't know well. In the middle of the night, they unknowingly get closer. What happens when they wake up?

ONLY ONE BODY

It's a rare romantasy that uses the Only One Body trope, maybe because it's challenging for two lovers to be so close. But the payoffs make this type of story worth exploring. This is like the Only One Bed trope, except instead of sharing a bedroom, your two lovers must share a body. Think of it as two souls in one. Either they jointly control the body, or they vie for control. Comedic hijinks are bound to occur in either scenario.

Only One Body stories mix well with other tropes. They might be Enemies to Lovers or Friends to Lovers. They might have Mutual Pining, which is bound to get complicated quickly. And if they aren't love interests for each other, then you've got the setup for an agonizing Love Triangle. Imagine they both fell for the same guy, but he didn't know about their Only One Body situation and therefore had no idea he was even in a love triangle???

They might be stuck together because of a spell, a curse, or a fissure in the space-time continuum. They're going to want to try to find a way out of their predicament. But by the time they finally break free from each other, will it feel like a victory or a tragic loss? Will they still be as close when they aren't literally so close to each other? Or will their feelings for each other change?

"Stop Trying to Control Me"

◆ SCENARIO ◆

Your protagonist and her best friend share a body. To operate this body, they must work together. If one wants to go somewhere the other one doesn't want to go, it can quickly turn into a tricky situation. A lot of compromises must be made. But what happens when one wants to go on a date, and the other isn't feeling it?

◆ BRAINSTORM ◆

Let's say the best friend is in love with your protagonist. He doesn't want your protagonist to go on this date because he's jealous. Think of several ways he might physically stop this body from moving. Watch old Charlie Chaplin clips and analyze how he moves—they might help you find language to describe the isolated and specific movements your main characters make when struggling to control their shared body.

◆ WRITE ◆

Write a scene where your protagonist tries to go on this date, but her best friend (who she's sharing a body with) won't let her go. This should anger your protagonist. The angrier she gets, the harder she fights back. Let this devolve into a scene of high physical comedy. Give them a hilarious assortment of blunders and awkward moves.

Remember: Sharing a body with someone is hard. It's physically exhausting and there's an emotional toll. Your protagonist is going through a lot! Her emotions might be quick to come to the surface.

◆ OPTIONAL ELEMENTS TO INCLUDE ◆

- Your protagonist nearly accidentally strangles herself.
- Someone observes your protagonist bickering with herself and thinks something is wrong with her.
- A moment where your protagonist almost gives up on the date, then decides she won't be thwarted this easily.

124 ✦ Write a Romantasy

Callbacks

Find a few physical movements you can use to establish a shorthand for their respective emotional states. Set up a few of these movements earlier, so you can use them to comedic effect in this scene.

"Oh, That's How I Know You"

◆ SCENARIO ◆

Your protagonist must share a body with a stranger after a spell gone wrong. They bicker as they get to know each other. Your protagonist has a nagging feeling she knows her new body-mate. She's fixated on finding an answer.

◆ BRAINSTORM ◆

Can they hear each other's thoughts, or do they need to speak to communicate? Does one of them speak while the other one thinks? Figure out the mechanics of this body time-share.

What if one of them has a problem with intimacy? They're independent, self-sufficient, and like being single. How would they deal with sharing a *body* with someone? This is worse than a normal roommate situation where it gets awkward having to share a bathroom. Sharing a body is much trickier, physically, mentally, and emotionally.

◆ WRITE ◆

Your protagonist suddenly remembers how she knows this guy she's sharing a body with. It's someone who did her wrong. And she absolutely *hates* him. Write the scene where she confronts him about his past misdeeds.

◆ OPTIONAL ELEMENTS TO INCLUDE ◆

- It feels like all hope is lost.
- He gaslights her.
- She tries to hurt him by hitting herself.

Fantasy Twist

If this is the result of a spell gone wrong, what's the antidote? Are they stuck like this forever or is there a way out?

"Give Me My Body Back, You Body-Stealing Troll"

◆ SCENARIO ◆

Your characters live in a world where body swapping is commonplace. Souls can pass from one body to another—with permission. But your protagonist's body was taken from her. She now resides in a body she doesn't want. And she's hunting for her original body. When she finds it, there will be hell to pay.

◆ BRAINSTORM ◆

What if body swapping was a science-tested activity that could be done relatively easily, like from a kiosk at an outdoor mall next to those weird massage chairs? What would the process look like? How long would it take? Would people have to sign waivers? Would you go into a booth? Would you stand in a futuristic cylinder? Come up with rules for how this would work.

◆ WRITE ◆

Write a scene where your protagonist finds her body. She gets into a heated argument with the person who commandeered her physical form. At first, she asks politely, but things turn ugly. As their fight escalates, your protagonist attacks her own body and finds her soul transporting. It works! She's back inside herself! Except wait . . . the guy who stole her body is still in here. How do you evict a spirit from inside yourself? And what happens when you start to get to know the guy . . . and you discover you *really* like him?

Remember: She's been looking for her body for a long time. When she finally encounters herself, it should feel like finding the Holy Grail.

◆ OPTIONAL ELEMENTS TO INCLUDE ◆

- A slap in the face.
- The harshest diss you can come up with.
- A moment where your protagonist thinks she's alone in her body, but she's wrong.

Fantasy Twist

Think about how it would feel to share your body with another soul. Does it tickle? What physical sensations feel different now, especially when the other person is the one at the reins?

Quick Writes

Set a timer for 15 minutes and do not stop writing until the timer goes off. Do not edit, cross out, or censor yourself. Write down every thought that comes to you.

1. Write a scene where a god/sorcerer tries to take over a human's body entirely but then discovers they're sharing the body instead.

2. Write a scene where your protagonist discovers her lover is dying. She meets with a doctor to get more information about body-sharing prospects.

3. Write a scene where your protagonist goes on a date with two people sharing the same body—but she doesn't know until halfway through the date. How does she find out?

4. Write a scene where two souls stuck in the same body get into an argument about where they're going out tonight. They both try to control where their body's going.

5. You've got two souls sharing a body—happily. Write a scene where one soul is violently ripped out of that body. The one who remains must find their missing other half.

Hidden Power/ The Chosen One

Your protagonist always thought she was ordinary. She may have been raised in poverty, on the outskirts of society. Or maybe she's an orphan. Or she comes from a working family that didn't have time to cultivate the talents of young ones.

Even though your protagonist lives a small life, she has big dreams. She looks at the world around her (whether that's Earth or a universe of your own invention), and she's horrified by the corruption and abuses of power she sees. She wishes she could change the world for the better, but it doesn't occur to her that she has the potential to make a difference.

Little does she know that she has something special inside. A Hidden Power. But it will soon be revealed. As she discovers what she can do, she'll become the heroine she was always destined to be.

As your protagonist grows into her powers, the dynamics in her romantic relationships will change. Your protagonist will need a love interest who isn't intimidated by greatness. The journey they take together is the path you create for the Hidden Power to unfold.

"Everything You Need Is Here"

◆ SCENARIO ◆

What if you learned you're The Chosen One, but nothing changed? You might wonder, *Did they make a mistake? How can I save the world if I have no special powers?* Maybe you worry there's something defective about your body. Then again, you've been told you're The Chosen One, so maybe it's possible to be powerful without powers? Unfortunately, your boyfriend or husband or partner or lover is trying to gaslight you into believing that isn't possible.

◆ BRAINSTORM ◆

How do supernatural characters acquire their powers? Do some freewriting to come up with different ideas about how your protagonist might defeat whatever bad guy she faces. If she doesn't possess "super" powers, what other internal powers might she have that would give her an advantage against her greatest enemies?

◆ WRITE ◆

Your protagonist is about to set out on a journey—she's been tasked with solving a seemingly unsolvable problem (anything from defeating a monster to saving the entire world). And she's ready for this! She wants to be The One! She thought she'd have some supernatural powers to help her, but maybe that's not in the cards.

Write a scene where your protagonist's lover tries to convince her she isn't capable of greatness—so your protagonist dumps him. Eff that noise. There's someone out there who will love her the way she deserves. Until she finds him, she can believe in herself. Maybe everything she needs to save the world is already inside her.

◆ OPTIONAL ELEMENTS TO INCLUDE ◆

- A tearful goodbye.
- A false start.
- A moment of destruction.

Callbacks

This isn't the first time your protagonist's partner has tried to gaslight her into believing she isn't enough. When she breaks up with him, she should have plenty of receipts.

"Wanna See Something Special?"

◆ SCENARIO ◆

Your protagonist recently came into her powers. She used to be average and suddenly, just like that, she's special. Different. She's really feeling the "super" part of being supernatural. Maybe it's even going to her head a little bit.

◆ BRAINSTORM ◆

Think of "coming into your powers" as a form of puberty. What changes might happen in your body? Are they noticeable or internal? Do powers make you feel different? Would your personality change? Would you treat your loved ones differently? Brainstorm how these powers might affect your protagonist.

◆ WRITE ◆

It's time for some fun and games. Write a scene where your protagonist experiments with her powers. This could be one scene or a series of scenes. Maybe she shows off to make an ex or a former friend jealous. Or maybe there's something she wants but can't afford, and she uses her powers to take it. Or perhaps she uses her powers while being intimate with her lover, to heighten the experience.

◆ OPTIONAL ELEMENTS TO INCLUDE ◆

- Flight.
- A moment of invisibility.
- The sound of chains breaking.

Fantasy Twist

Is it possible to use a superpower too much? What if your protagonist burns out her powers before she's had a chance to use them the way they were intended?

" It's Time for You to Accept Who You Are "

◆ SCENARIO ◆

What if you were destined to save the world, but you didn't want to? Not in a selfish way, more in an oh-my-God-what-if-I-mess-this-up-and-get-everyone-killed kind of way. That's a lot of pressure. You might want to scream to the gods, "Choose anyone other than me!" But that's not the deal. You have been chosen. And now it's time to step up and settle into your role.

◆ BRAINSTORM ◆

Make a list of all the reasons your protagonist wouldn't want to be a leader. It can be a pros and cons list. Then make another list of all the reasons your protagonist *needs* this.

◆ WRITE ◆

Write a scene where your protagonist's lover convinces her to accept her destiny. They might be in bed together, postcoitus. Your protagonist is feeling vulnerable. She wants to give up, to crawl into a hole and disappear. But her lover sees her for who she is. Her lover believes in her. And that belief is what finally convinces your protagonist.

◆ OPTIONAL ELEMENTS TO INCLUDE ◆

- Words of affirmation.
- A story from one of their childhoods.
- A mirror.
- A sign of good luck.

Fantasy Twist

What does it even mean to be chosen? Can your protagonist have a conversation with God, or with the gods? The more readers see your protagonist struggling with her role, the more satisfying it's going to be when she ultimately, proudly takes possession of her powers.

Quick Writes

Set a timer for 15 minutes and do not stop writing until the timer goes off. Do not edit, cross out, or censor yourself. Write down every thought that comes to you.

1. Your protagonist is afraid to be a leader. Write a scene where she does something drastic to try to reject her destiny.

2. A wise mentor is helping your protagonist learn how to harness her powers. Write a scene where your protagonist confides in a friend that she's falling in love with her mentor. She knows it's wrong, but she can't help herself.

3. Write a scene where your protagonist is captured by an enemy—but before she's taken away, she leaves a message behind for her lover.

4. Write a scene where your protagonist goes to a support group for other Chosen Ones who received their powers late in life.

5. Your protagonist has gotten cocky and overconfident since coming into her powers. Write a scene where her best friend and ally tries to get through to her. This friend doesn't want these new powers to corrupt your protagonist.

Time Travel

*T*he greatest way for readers to inject some excitement into their everyday lives is to get comfortable on the couch and sink deeply into a Time Travel romantasy. Do you feel like you were born in the right time? What eras do you wish you could experience firsthand? What dangers do you think you'd experience in the past? How about the future?

The trick of writing Time Travel is being very specific in the rules you establish. How do your characters make the big leap? Is it something scientific, like a time travel machine, or is it more magical, like a spell or a portal? Are they in control of their time jump, or does it happen to them? Do they know the destination they're going to, or is it a surprise when they get there? And maybe most importantly, do they know how to get back to the era they came from?

Answer these questions for yourself, then send your protagonist and her love interest on a wild adventure through time. If you're a writer who loves research, this is a great trope to explore. Historically authentic details will make your book come to life.

"It Was You"

◆ SCENARIO ◆

Your protagonist goes back into the not-so-distant past to change something. (You decide what.) She's careful not to be seen, but one person witnesses her in the moment of either arrival or departure. Now, in the present day, your protagonist meets (and falls in love with) her witness from the past. Your protagonist doesn't know she was seen by this person. But her witness recognizes her immediately. He just can't place where he's seen her before.

◆ BRAINSTORM ◆

What did your protagonist change in the past and why was it necessary? Was she going back into the past to right a wrong? Is there any way her witness might misinterpret what she did?

It can be easy to forget a stranger's face—but what about specific details like a hairstyle, an item of clothing, or how a person moves? What might your protagonist do to out themselves?

◆ WRITE ◆

Write the witness's "aha" moment. He tells himself what he saw must have been a figment of his imagination or a hallucination. When he realizes it was real, he'll want an explanation. Depending on how well your protagonist explains herself, this scene could bring them closer together or things could go off the rails, fast.

Remember: When writing a Time Travel story, you must create your own set of time-traveling rules and follow them strictly. Don't underestimate your readers—they'll catch you if you break the rules, and this could cause them to time travel away from the world of your story.

◆ OPTIONAL ELEMENTS TO INCLUDE ◆

- An expiration date.
- Disbelief.
- Denial.

Fantasy Twist

What if your protagonist doesn't succeed on her first trip back into the past? What if she must go back several times, and her witness sees her each time? How does each successive visit further cement his impression of your protagonist (even if each visit feels new to him)?

"You Don't Want to Go Where I've Been"

◆ SCENARIO ◆

Your protagonist is a seasoned time traveler, and each passage through time has a ripple effect. The ripples are different sizes, but every trip into the past has consequences. Just when your protagonist decides she's done, a lover asks for a favor: "Take me with you next time."

◆ BRAINSTORM ◆

Come up with a list of things that don't exist anymore because of your protagonist's interdimensional travels. It should be a mix of positive, negative, and neutral items. Your protagonist might have tried to stop something from happening and assumed she succeeded. But fate is fickle and some of the events that have been "deleted" from history were unstoppable. What happens when she realizes she didn't *actually* change history successfully? What are the repercussions in her romantic relationship?

◆ WRITE ◆

Write a scene where your protagonist says no. She won't, under any circumstances, take her lover into the past. It's too dangerous. She refuses to do it. But her lover is persistent and won't back down.

◆ OPTIONAL ELEMENTS TO INCLUDE ◆

- An emotional confession.
- An object from the past that no longer exists.

Callbacks

What if your protagonist made a promise to her lover in an earlier scene? A promise that he brings up now, to lay on the pressure.

"If You're Me, Then Who Am I?"

◆ SCENARIO ◆

Your protagonist must visit a moment from the beginning of her current relationship. She needs to deliver an important message to a slightly younger version of her lover. It's a tricky quest because what if she bumps into her younger self? That kind of encounter might alter the space-time continuum in a disastrous way. Two versions of the same person are not supposed to exist at the same time! And unfortunately for your protagonist, the thing she's trying hardest not to let happen is going to happen.

◆ BRAINSTORM ◆

What's going on in your protagonist's relationship now that would require a fix in the past? Come up with a reason she can't deny. What are the problems that most plague your protagonist and her partner? What do they fight about? What issues keep coming up over and over again? Think about the mistakes people make when they're young that haunt them later in life. Maybe she wants to save her relationship by righting a specific wrong from her past. Whatever the reason, it needs to be big enough that she would risk moving through time.

◆ WRITE ◆

Write a scene where your protagonist meets up with her lover in the past and then accidentally bumps into herself. Show your readers how careful she is to avoid this. But it doesn't matter. This moment is going to happen whether she likes it or not. Take the scene in an unexpected direction. Have her Past Self react in a way your readers don't see coming.

◆ OPTIONAL ELEMENTS TO INCLUDE ◆

- ♦ A startling moment of physical contact.
- ♦ A panic attack.
- ♦ A meaningful artifact.
- ♦ A secret comes to light unexpectedly.

Fantasy Twist

If you saw your Future Self, would you even believe it? Would you think at first that they were just a doppelgänger, someone who looks alarmingly like you? Would you be able to sense your innate selfhood within this other human? Think about how you would react and let that inform the reaction of your protagonist's Past Self.

Callbacks

What could your protagonist say to her Past Self to prove she's herself? Alternately, what might your protagonist say to trick her Past Self into believing she *isn't* the same person?

Quick Writes

Set a timer for 15 minutes and do not stop writing until the timer goes off. Do not edit, cross out, or censor yourself. Write down every thought that comes to you.

1. It's the present day. Your protagonist meets a time traveler from the distant past who is lost. They're clueless about our modern-day customs and they commit a faux pas that puts them in danger. Write a scene where your protagonist helps this wayward traveler.

2. Your protagonist is stuck in the past, where she's fallen in love. Write a scene where she turns down her one opportunity to go back to the present day because she won't leave her lover behind.

3. Write a scene where your protagonist meets a younger version of her love interest, and the interaction helps her understand something her love interest is struggling with in the present day.

4. Write a scene where your protagonist suddenly finds herself in a futuristic world where she's a wanted criminal. She immediately seeks out an ally to help her hide.

5. Write a scene where your protagonist is sent home to the present day without her love interest. Does she mourn her loss, or does she try to travel back in time again?

Meet-Cute

Some people say Meet-Cutes only happen in movies. But you never know . . . People do have Meet-Cutes in the real world. And these chance encounters bring a charmed-life sort of magic to romantasy.

The chance meeting could happen in so many ways:

- You reach for the last copy of the same book at your favorite indie bookshop, and after an adorable negotiation, you both decide on a joint custody agreement.
- You go to the same seat at the opera and have a playful argument about who's in the wrong place, then realize it's your mistake because you aren't wearing your glasses.
- You both get stuck without an umbrella, waiting out a storm under the same awning, and you get so lost in conversation that when it stops raining you don't even notice.

There's a secret about a Meet-Cute that gives it special meaning for your characters and your story. It always seems like an accident to the couple. But what your readers see is something far more romantic. Destiny. Only a quirk of fate can bring two people together like this. Now it's up to you to create a story that proves, in a dramatic and roundabout way, that this was meant to be.

"This Must Be Yours"

◆ SCENARIO ◆

Your protagonist accidentally retrieves the wrong package. She gets all the way home before she sees what's inside. And oh, wow, it's not what she was waiting for. She checks the outside of the package, sees another person's name. And an address. Looks like she has another errand to run.

◆ BRAINSTORM ◆

What's the worst thing your protagonist could find in the box? Come up with ten possibilities. Get more embarrassing as you list them. Conversely, what's in your protagonist's missing package? Make it something she urgently needs.

◆ WRITE ◆

Write the scene where your protagonist returns the package. She's hoping this guy has her missing item and they can swap. He doesn't. (This gives you more places to go with the story.) He's mortified she saw his package—and offers to help her find hers, which will give him time to explain himself. Thus begins a day of misadventure . . .

Remember: These characters are going to fall in love. Before that happens, you want your readers to root for your protagonist and this guy to get together. Whatever's inside the box shouldn't be creepy or gross. Creepy isn't cute, but awkward is.

◆ OPTIONAL ELEMENTS TO INCLUDE ◆

- He laughs nervously whenever he's embarrassed.
- A running gag where he tries to convince her that the package doesn't belong to him.
- The package explodes or disappears.
- Someone steals his package, so now they have two packages to retrieve.

Fantasy Twist

What if the thing inside the box is alive? What if it's from another planet? What if it's a collection of ingredients intended for a strange (possibly life-altering) spell? What if it's haunted, cursed, or contains dark magic? There are so many interesting directions you could go with this reveal. Let your imagination run wild. Outside-the-box thinking only, please.

"Do You Think It's Broken?"

◆ SCENARIO ◆

Your protagonist had a bad morning. Everything that could go wrong has gone wrong. Now she's late for an important meeting/interview/battle. As she races through town on foot, she dodges obstacles. Almost colliding into a man, nearly smacking into a woman, coming close to running another person over. But instead of having her Meet-Cute, she sees two *other* people colliding.

◆ BRAINSTORM ◆

Write your protagonist's inner monologue as she runs. What will happen if she's late? Maybe she must prove herself today or she'll face major consequences. Get into her head to understand the stakes.

◆ WRITE ◆

Okay, so your protagonist sees these strangers colliding. In another story, that would be someone else's Meet-Cute. But one of the people in the collision takes off, leaving the other person on the ground. Your protagonist shouldn't stop. She should ignore that stranger, even though he's clearly injured. She's late! But she's a good person, so she goes to help. Write that scene.

◆ OPTIONAL ELEMENTS TO INCLUDE ◆

- A touch that lingers too long.
- A comically broken limb.
- Your protagonist faints.

Fantasy Twist

Can your protagonist use a healing spell to help this stranger? What if she gets the spell wrong and accidentally makes things worse for him?

"Haven't We Met Before?"

◆ SCENARIO ◆

"Haven't we met before?" It's a straightforward question. But the answer can go in so many different directions.

- "Yes, but I wish we hadn't."
- "No, but I wish we had."
- "Yes, and I'm sorry I was so mean to you."

And so on. Well, your protagonist is about to bump into someone from her past and he's gonna ask that question. There is no way in hell she's going to tell him the truth.

◆ BRAINSTORM ◆

Come up with an exceptionally unusual Meet-Cute for this scene. The weirder the better. As a quick exercise, jot down a list of places where someone is least likely to meet the love of their life, like the DMV or the bottom of a well. There is no place too unlikely, terrible, or extreme.

◆ WRITE ◆

Your protagonist has a Meet-Cute, which leads to a phone number exchange. When she enters this guy's number in her phone, his name pops up. How is that possible? Then it all comes crashing back: She knows this guy. They went on one date, years ago. It went well. So well it was the kind of date you tell your grandkids about. Except your protagonist wasn't ready for a commitment, so she ghosted him. Back to their current Meet-Cute: He doesn't recognize her yet, but he's bound to remember at some point. Can she get away with never telling him the truth?

Remember: Build a sense of foreboding into this scene. When the truth is ultimately revealed, your reader will want to reread this scene to see how badly your protagonist handled this new beginning.

◆ OPTIONAL ELEMENTS TO INCLUDE ◆

- A rejected compliment, given twice.
- A moment of laughter.
- A promise.

Callbacks

Think about the last time these two characters were in contact. Maybe your protagonist says something here that seems familiar to the love interest, but he can't quite place it. Yet.

Quick Writes

Set a timer for 15 minutes and do not stop writing until the timer goes off. Do not edit, cross out, or censor yourself. Write down every thought that comes to you.

1. Write a scene where your protagonist bumps into a handsome stranger in a magic shop. They knock over an elixir. It causes one of them to transform in an eye-popping way.

2. Write a series of scenes where your protagonist has several Meet-Cutes in one day. With so many crushable new love interests, who's she supposed to end up with?

3. Write a scene where your protagonist has a Meet-Cute before departing on a long trip. What if this is The One and she leaves him before they've had a chance to fall in love?

4. Write a scene where your protagonist rants to her BFF about hating the idea of Meet-Cutes, then follow that with an immediate, irresistible Meet-Cute scene.

5. Write a Meet-Cute where your protagonist accidentally rips her blouse (perhaps during an unfortunate encounter with a dragon or other creature) and then a stranger literally gives her the shirt off his back. Hello, handsome.

Meet-Ugly

If your main couple excitedly tells everyone at a dinner party the story of how they met, they probably had a Meet-Cute. But if they clam up, focus intensely on their food, and mumble under their breath, "Please dear God, don't ask us how we met each other," then it's more likely they had a Meet-Ugly. This is the Meet-Cute's crazy cousin. There is nothing adorable about meeting this way, at least not for the two people involved.

Some potential Meet-Ugly scenarios: Your protagonist is drunk, she throws up on a stranger, then asks for his number. Your protagonist just got dumped, she can't stop crying, she tries to steal a box of Kleenex from the store, gets caught, then the guard takes pity on her and lets her go, but only if she agrees to go out for coffee. Your protagonist is the first colonizer on a distant moon, where she accidentally destroys a precious resource and awakens a long-hibernating alien lifeform who takes her as a human concubine—and sparks fly.

Let your characters be complicated, flawed, and painfully human (even if they aren't actually human).

"You've Got to Be Kidding Me"

◆ SCENARIO ◆

Things aren't going well for your protagonist. Life is a never-ending string of loss, despair, betrayal. One bad thing after another. Just when she thinks nothing else could possibly go wrong, worse things happen. It's as if her misfortune was written in the stars.

◆ BRAINSTORM ◆

Come up with ten events/moments from your protagonist's recent past that she would consider bad luck. Anything from minor inconveniences to full-on tragedies. When your protagonist strings all these events together, it feels like she's been cursed. Does she believe in luck? If not, does she have any other theories about why so much has gone wrong for her? How does this affect the way she sees the world? Is she ever optimistic or does life just get her down?

◆ WRITE ◆

Write a scene where your protagonist complains to her best friend about her doomed life and nonexistent romantic prospects. The friend gives her a pep talk. Just as she starts to feel better, a disastrous event occurs that literally drops a life-changing love interest in her lap.

Remember: Be creative with this disastrous event. What if the ceiling caves in, bringing a man with it? Or her shuttle makes an emergency landing and another passenger who wasn't strapped in clings to your protagonist for survival as they crash? Or a mudslide pushes a stranger's home into your protagonist's living room, along with a handsome neighbor? The more outrageous, the better.

◆ OPTIONAL ELEMENTS TO INCLUDE ◆

- Curious onlookers who don't offer to help.
- An item of clothing that must be removed.
- A resurrection of some sort.

Fantasy Twist

What if your protagonist thinks the event is a natural disaster, but the truth is it was caused by her love interest? He was using supernatural powers. How might your protagonist react when she finds out?

"I Don't Hate You, I Detest You—And Yes, There's a Difference"

◆ SCENARIO ◆

Your protagonist has a very messy, very emotional, very public breakup. She expresses years of pent-up emotion. It's the kind of breakup that buzzes with finality. Your protagonist is dropping a nuclear bomb on her love life. There's no going back now.

◆ BRAINSTORM ◆

In what ways was this relationship toxic? And what drove your protagonist over the edge? Get inside her head, writing from her point of view about why she had to get out so desperately.

◆ WRITE ◆

Write a post-breakup scene where a stranger who witnessed the big emotional showdown shows her kindness, taking care of her in a small but important way. Maybe it's an offer of tissues, or a cup of water, or a promise that "it'll be okay." This is the worst moment for your protagonist to meet someone. But there's something about this stranger . . .

◆ OPTIONAL ELEMENTS TO INCLUDE ◆

- Uncontrollable tears.
- An embarrassingly snotty used tissue.
- A firm embrace.

Fantasy Twist

What if this stranger's pheromones calm your protagonist? He's a different species, from a different world. Your protagonist can't help but be drawn to this stranger's essence.

"Why Would You Ever Think I'd Like That?"

◆ SCENARIO ◆

Your protagonist has a customer service job. Maybe she works in android sales, or she's a barkeep at an inn on the outskirts of a woodsy town, or she's a curse breaker with a small souvenir store. She's dealing with an angry customer who is increasingly rude. You decide what that looks like, but one thing is certain: This is about to get ugly.

◆ BRAINSTORM ◆

How does your protagonist normally diffuse tension? Imagine she's running a customer service seminar where she talks through her best practices in tricky scenarios. Does she follow her own advice? What would she do if things escalated to a point where she couldn't control the situation? Make a list of the protocols she'd usually (at least try to) follow.

◆ WRITE ◆

Write a scene where a belligerent customer threatens your protagonist. She can handle herself until things escalate. Another customer helps . . . and gets beaten to a bloody pulp. Your protagonist tends to his injuries and she's shocked to discover that she's attracted to her unsuccessful savior.

Remember: This is a Meet-Ugly, so make the love interest's injuries bloody! The bloodier the better. From now on, every time they see blood, these two lovers will think about the moment they met.

◆ OPTIONAL ELEMENTS TO INCLUDE ◆

- Someone gets thrown through a window.
- Your protagonist slips in a puddle of her love interest's blood.
- A stranger passes out.

Fantasy Twist

The love interest has self-healing powers, but they work slowly. The good news: He won't die in your protagonist's arms. The better news: She gets to play Florence Nightingale for the night.

Callbacks

This doesn't have to be the only time your characters encounter this angry, violent customer. How might a second encounter with this customer later in your story affect them?

Quick Writes

Set a timer for 15 minutes and do not stop writing until the timer goes off. Do not edit, cross out, or censor yourself. Write down every thought that comes to you.

1. Write a scene where your protagonist searches for an accidentally discarded family heirloom at the dump. A handsome worker helps her search. Sparks fly between them, despite the stench.

2. Write a scene where your protagonist gets stuck in quicksand. A hot stranger tries to help, but he starts to sink too. If they get out of this alive, this will be such a great story!

3. Write a scene where your protagonist is taken captive by pirates and locks eyes with another prisoner while they're walking adjacent planks. Could this be love?

4. Your protagonist is searching for meaning in her life. Write a scene where she has too much to drink and gets violently ill all over her guru/love interest.

5. Write a scene where your protagonist has a terrible allergic reaction to her blind date. Little does she know, her date is a(n) [insert mythical creature of your choice here].

STAR-CROSSED LOVERS

*I*t's one thing when your parents, or perhaps society, are against your relationship. (See the Forbidden Love chapter.) But what if the whole universe is against it? What if a seer instructs you and your lover to avoid each other? What if it's written in the stars that your coupling can't continue? Will you listen to these super-powerful forces or to your heart?

Star-Crossed Lovers refuse to heed these warning signs. Star-Crossed Lovers defy anyone who orders them to stay apart. Star-Crossed Lovers are too passionate to deny their love!

This is a bigger risk than simply breaking a social contract and straying from cultural norms. Their love could destroy empires or galaxies. It could end life as we know it. When the gods have a personal stake in the outcome of your love life, you don't want to make them angry. But if you get your readers invested in this relationship, they'll root for your protagonists regardless of the repercussions. If it means these characters can finally find happiness, it'll all be worth it.

"Do You Believe in Destiny?"

◆ SCENARIO ◆

Your protagonist keeps having the same dream. She sees herself happy, in love, and living the life she's always envisioned. The person she's with in these dreams is always the same, but she doesn't recognize him. Is it someone created by her subconscious? Perhaps a facsimile of faces she's seen before? Then one day as she walks through the center of her village, guess who she sees?

◆ BRAINSTORM ◆

Write this dream in vivid detail. You might not use the dream in your story, but it will be helpful to have a sense of how the dream transpires. Come up with several images from it. Don't worry about making sense. Dream logic is fine.

◆ WRITE ◆

Write a scene where your protagonist sees the person from her dreams and introduces herself. Something to consider: Has this other character also seen your protagonist in his dreams?

Here's a secret for your protagonist: The dream always ends badly, but she chooses to ignore that and focus on how this person makes her feel. Could she have those feelings for real? Is this destiny?

◆ OPTIONAL ELEMENTS TO INCLUDE ◆

- A repeated line of dialogue.
- A surprising display of emotion.
- Their conversation is abruptly halted by a nearby disaster/catastrophe.

Fantasy Twist

How can you heighten this moment in a way that makes it feel pre-ordained? Do the animals in the area start acting strange, like when there's about to be an earthquake? Are there unusual changes in the weather? Does the sky suddenly, actually start falling?

Callbacks

Are there any other specific details from her dreams that come into play when they meet? Create a sense of déjà vu for the characters and your readers.

"Nobody Understands Me Like You Do"

◆ SCENARIO ◆

Your protagonist and her lover were forcibly separated. She doesn't know where he was taken or if he's alive. She's desperate to find him. The uncertainty is driving her crazy, but then she receives a secret message from her lover with instructions. He's giving her a way to find him—a road map with clues only she would be able to decipher. It's a glimmer of hope.

◆ BRAINSTORM ◆

Who kidnapped the love interest, where did they take him, and why? Whoever took him wants to keep these two characters apart for good, so think about how hard it was for him to communicate with your protagonist. He took great pains to do this. How did he manage it? Does anyone else know about the message? What problems might that raise later in your story?

◆ WRITE ◆

Write a scene where your protagonist is about to give up and do something drastic in despair, but then this message from her lover arrives. How does she react? Is she so thrilled she almost puts him in danger by excitedly telling someone about the letter? Or does she immediately lock into stealth mode and begin plotting how to use this new information to rescue him?

◆ OPTIONAL ELEMENTS TO INCLUDE ◆

- If there's a physical letter, part of it has gotten wet (or torn) and is therefore illegible.
- The person who delivers the message demands payment from your protagonist.
- The message self-destructs.

Fantasy Twist

The message could take many forms: a written letter, a hologram, an audio recording. The love interest is worried about his message getting intercepted, so he uses a code. He might include references to their relationship that only your protagonist (and your readers) would understand. Or maybe he uses a secret language to keep your protagonist safe.

"Let's Leave Tonight"

◆ SCENARIO ◆

It feels like everyone's trying to pressure your protagonist and her lover into breaking up. They're getting it from every direction. No one seems to understand that this isn't going to happen. There's only one way they can escape all the noise: run away.

◆ BRAINSTORM ◆

Why don't people approve of their love? Whose voice do they immediately discard? Who are they most likely to listen to? Is anyone able to move them to a sense of doubt? List as many supporting characters as you can; brainstorm how you think they'd each feel in this scenario.

◆ WRITE ◆

Your protagonist and her lover are packing their bags. They're planning to leave in the dead of night. But one of them has second thoughts. What if this is a bad idea? Write a scene where they debate the pros and cons of leaving. By the end of the scene, they've made a firm decision.

◆ OPTIONAL ELEMENTS TO INCLUDE ◆

- A frantic kiss.
- They ignore a warning.
- A tearful goodbye with a neighbor.

Fantasy Twist

Even if they're able to leave, how might their destiny follow them? Can you really run away from fate? Think about the consequences of their decision—are they physical, spiritual, magical, or something else?

Quick Writes

Set a timer for 15 minutes and do not stop writing until the timer goes off. Do not edit, cross out, or censor yourself. Write down every thought that comes to you.

1. Write a scene where a seer visits your main couple and predicts violence in their future. They do not react well.//
2. Write a scene where your protagonist breaks up with her lover to keep him safe from a prophecy—she's pushing him away to protect him.
3. Write a scene where your main couple faces a tribunal that banishes them from this world to protect others from the doom their love may cause.
4. Write a tearful monologue for one of your main protagonists as they lament the way others have treated them. How can love be wrong?
5. Your protagonist tries to trick the gods—she and her best friend swap identities to hide the fact that she's coupled in a doomed love affair. Write a scene where she gets caught.

Childhood Sweethearts

No one knows you quite like your childhood best friend. You've been inseparable for so long it feels like they're an extension of you. They've seen you at your petulant worst. They know your hopes and dreams because they were with you when you were figuring out who you were and who you wanted to become. You're protective of each other in a way no one else can be. Are you secretly a vampire, an Amazonian warrior trapped in the wrong world, or a vengeance demon in human form? Your childhood bestie will keep your secret.

This relationship goes deeper than your average Friends to Lovers story because Childhood Sweethearts are sort of like twins. When you hurt, they hurt. When you win, they win. What they love, you love. Their enemies are your enemies. Even before you develop romantic feelings for each other, you're already two halves of a whole.

One fun thing about writing a Childhood Sweethearts story is you have so many opportunities for flashbacks. These characters have history—use it. Dig back into their formative years. Make your readers feel like these characters are their childhood besties too.

"It's You, It's Always Been You"

◆ SCENARIO ◆

Your protagonist is betrothed to someone she doesn't love. She agreed to this marriage to broker peace between two families, two empires, two worlds. But as the epic wedding ceremony begins, all she can think about is her best friend watching from the pews. He's the one she wants.

◆ BRAINSTORM ◆

Think about how much pressure your protagonist feels. How much emotion has she pushed down to let herself get here? Does she have *any* feelings for the person she's marrying, or is it all a sham? Has she told anyone her true feelings, or is she lying even to herself? Think through her complicated headspace as she walks down the aisle.

◆ WRITE ◆

Write a scene where your protagonist objects to her own wedding. What kind of chaos transpires as she makes a declaration of love for the friend who's always been there for her, and who she knows will be there for her in the wake of this mess. True love is worth the repercussions she's going to face after this very public change of heart.

Remember: Your protagonist will have friends, family, and allies here—and possibly enemies as well. And even if she didn't have enemies before the ceremony, her speech will create some. Think about how much danger her love creates for herself and her childhood best friend. This may not have been the wisest thing to do, but she had to follow her heart. Make her pay for it.

◆ OPTIONAL ELEMENTS TO INCLUDE ◆

- ◆ A ripped gown.
- ◆ Chaos, screams, confusion.
- ◆ A vow of revenge.

Fantasy Twist

Think about the stakes of this aborted wedding. How big can you make the fallout of this choice, not only for your protagonist but also for her community? Let it have far-reaching consequences that affect the entire world of your story. Everyone's fate is tied to this impulsive action.

"You Make Me Want to Be Better Than I Am"

◆ SCENARIO ◆

Your protagonist has done something stupid. She's made a huge mistake. It's up to you to decide what she did, but a few of just some of the possibilities include selling something that belonged to her lover to pay off a debt, betraying her lover's trust (either cheating or a lesser offense), letting loose an age-old curse, making a deal with a devil, or indulging in an illegal substance she promised to give up. Whatever she's done, her lover—the one she's known since youth—is pissed, and he's not sure he can forgive her.

◆ BRAINSTORM ◆

Has your protagonist ever messed up *this* badly? Think about what creates higher stakes for your couple. If this is a first, what caused her to lose her way? If it's the fiftieth time, why can't she stop? Does she ever think about how her actions affect her lover? Why or why not?

◆ WRITE ◆

Write a scene where your protagonist asks for forgiveness. Her lover knows her flaws all too well and he's forgiven her before, so she's hopeful. But as she allows herself to be vulnerable, she looks into his eyes and gets scared. Will he accept her apology, or has she gone too far? If he does forgive her, make her work for it.

Remember: These characters are Childhood Sweethearts, which means they know each other's families. What if your troubled protagonist reaches out to someone in her love interest's family for advice?

◆ OPTIONAL ELEMENTS TO INCLUDE ◆

- Your protagonist rushes her words.
- The love interest has a confession of his own.
- They are interrupted by an emergency alert.

Fantasy Twist

Your protagonist is so nervous about how her lover will react that she seeks advice from a seer. But maybe the seer's prophecies are foggy and confusing. Maybe they make things worse.

"Do You Remember the Day We Met?"

◆ SCENARIO ◆

They were each other's first everything. First crush, first kiss, first sex. Also, first breakup. But that didn't end their friendship. Over the years, they've been by each other's side through life's crazy ups and downs. And it's finally dawning on your protagonist: She's in love with her best friend. Could he possibly feel the same?

◆ BRAINSTORM ◆

These two characters have grown closer and closer through the years—so what is it about this moment that's different? What's happened to make your protagonist finally see her childhood friend in a new (or old) light? Think about all the beats that have led her to this place. Does he see things in the same way? Think about why or why not.

◆ WRITE ◆

Write a scene where your protagonist declares her love. Make it hard for her to get this out because she's nervous about her friend's reaction. She might reference her first impression from the day they met, or maybe she even has an object she's held on to that she brings out in this scene. Something her friend gave her years ago that she's kept as a sort of talisman.

◆ OPTIONAL ELEMENTS TO INCLUDE ◆

- A false start.
- Her friend knows what she's going to say before she even says it.
- An inside joke.

Fantasy Twist

What otherworldly threat might make it urgent for your protagonist to confess her love? Does she see an army of flying dragons heading her way? Is there an alien spaceship overhead? Does a portal open up in the sky as she prepares to speak? It's now or never.

Callbacks

Think about how romantic it feels when you realize that someone sees you clearly and loves you for who you truly are. As your protagonist expresses her love, have her use specific details about moments over the years when her feelings for her friend deepened.

Quick Writes

Set a timer for 15 minutes and do not stop writing until the timer goes off. Do not edit, cross out, or censor yourself. Write down every thought that comes to you.

1. Write a scene where your protagonist finds a letter she wrote to her childhood best friend when she was eight. Her youthful thoughts bring clarity to their current relationship.

2. Your protagonist and her lover have broken up. When they show up separately at a wedding or funeral, mutual friends and loved ones swarm around them protectively. How do they take charge of this awkward situation? Is reconciliation in the air?

3. Write a flashback scene that shows the first time these two characters met in childhood. Include an element of foreboding: Something about their world is about to collapse. But we know from their instant connection that they will help each other through this.

4. Write a flashback scene where your protagonist and her best friend make a pact that one of them is destined to break later in your story.

5. Your protagonist and her best friend live in a colony on a desolate planet. One is offered a job (and a better life) in a faraway galaxy. Can they go together or is this the end?

I Have a Secret

"There's something you need to know. Something I've been keeping from you, but I can't hold it in anymore: I Have a Secret. If I tell you what it is, do you promise not to tell anyone?"

There's nothing like a secret to keep your readers guessing. It could be a secret one of your characters guards intensely. Or it could be a secret about one of the characters that you, the writer, are keeping from your readers. You might clue your readers into the fact that one of your characters is hiding something but hold off on revealing the secret itself. Build that anticipation and your readers will have to turn the pages to find out more.

The prompts in this chapter deal with secrets that will be incorporated into the plot of your story, but another fun exercise to play is to give every character a secret, even if your readers won't learn most of them. You want your supporting characters to feel as rich and complicated as your main protagonists. Because don't we all have a secret or two?

Remember, a secret has more power when it's being withheld from someone, so take time revealing what your characters are keeping quiet.

"Can I Trust You?"

◆ SCENARIO ◆

This relationship is new. And your protagonist has a huge secret. The kind of secret that could get her killed. She's been alone with this secret for so long that she's desperate to talk about it, and she's starting to wonder, *Is this the person I share it with?*

◆ BRAINSTORM ◆

Think about what your protagonist's secret is and who else it involves. Who would want to hurt her for this information? There should be real stakes in her not wanting to get caught, so think about the repercussions. How much danger is she in?

◆ WRITE ◆

Write a scene where the love interest confronts your protagonist. He's concerned she's shying away, and that she's holding something back. She doesn't know how to react: Does he genuinely care for her and want to help, or could he be associated with her enemy? You decide if she reveals her secret or not.

◆ OPTIONAL ELEMENTS TO INCLUDE ◆

- A treasured and weathered photo from her past.
- A happy anecdote from your protagonist's childhood.
- A move to a private location.

Callbacks

Write a quick scene flashing back to the moment where your protagonist first acquired her secret. What did she do or see that she can't tell anyone about? Make it visceral and raw.

"I'll Tell You Mine If You Tell Me Yours"

◆ SCENARIO ◆

Your protagonist and her lover are still getting to know each other. They have an incredible physical connection, but they've been slower to trust each other with their feelings. It seems the emotional shields they each wear are much harder to strip away than their clothing.

◆ BRAINSTORM ◆

Everyone has different types of secrets, from silly to deeply serious. Come up with three secrets for your protagonist and three secrets for her lover. Give each secret a menu rating: mild, medium, or spicy. How closely do they guard each one?

◆ WRITE ◆

Write a postcoital scene where these characters flirtatiously trade secrets. You decide how far they're willing to go with each other, and why. At least one of them should hold a secret back.

◆ OPTIONAL ELEMENTS TO INCLUDE ◆

♦ A gentle nudge.
♦ Instant regret.
♦ One of them gets caught in a lie.

Fantasy Twist

Think about how secrets are used as currency. What if one of the shared secrets could be traded for some sort of supernatural power? If they're willing to break their lover's trust, that is.

"Who Else Have You Told?"

◆ SCENARIO ◆

Your protagonist and her lover have a power imbalance. He might be her boss, or he's the commander of your protagonist's squadron of rebel fighters, or he has supernatural powers that she lacks. Which is why she doesn't go to him immediately when she finds out she's pregnant.

◆ BRAINSTORM ◆

Has the love interest ever said or done anything to make your protagonist feel alone or separate? Examine the lowest points of their relationship. Even if he didn't mean to make her feel "less than," status inequalities within a couple can affect their dynamic. Think about moments when he made her think, *We aren't the same.*

◆ WRITE ◆

Write a scene where your protagonist asks a friend for advice and reveals her secret pregnancy. The friend urges her not to tell anyone. This might be terrible advice (and the friend might have ulterior motives), but your protagonist doesn't know what to do, so she stays silent.

Remember: Your protagonist can't keep this secret forever. What's her plan for when she starts to show? Does her friend help her figure out how to continue hiding her pregnancy? Does she have to disappear? What will she do next?

◆ OPTIONAL ELEMENTS TO INCLUDE ◆

- Happy tears.
- An unexpected gift.
- Your protagonist doesn't know it, but someone is spying on her.

Fantasy Twist

If the love interest has special powers your protagonist doesn't possess, would their child have these same abilities? How might that affect her pregnancy? What if her body undergoes unusual changes? By keeping quiet, is she putting herself in physical danger? How will her lover feel when he finally finds out?

Quick Writes

Set a timer for 15 minutes and do not stop writing until the timer goes off. Do not edit, cross out, or censor yourself. Write down every thought that comes to you.

1. Your protagonist has secretly given birth to a child with special powers. Write a scene where she discovers what this child can do.

2. Your protagonist's love interest is secretly a werewolf/vampire/demon (or another mythical creature). Write a spicy scene where he accidentally transforms in the middle of sex.

3. Your protagonist is secretly the heir to a great fortune. Write a scene where her lover confronts her about where she gets all her money.

4. Write a scene where your protagonist learns she was adopted—her birth parents are from another world, they're evil, and they're trying to find her.

5. Your protagonist suspects her lover is living a double life. Write a series of scenes where she tries to find proof by going through his things and following him.

Fake Relationship

Some people say that if you stare deeply into someone's eyes long enough, you're bound to fall in love. You can find a quiz online that claims to be a recipe for love—sit with someone for 10 minutes and answer each question and by the time you finish you'll be soulmates. Both ideas have an underlying "fake-it-'til-you-make-it" vibe. Love is an action you can perform; it's something you can make out of nothing.

That's what makes the Fake Relationship trope so satisfying. There's so much joy in seeing two people go from merely needing each other (for a green card, to appease a strict parent) to genuinely needing each other (because of full-blown, raging love). Every step of the way, there are opportunities to keep your readers guessing about what's real and what's not as the chemistry between your couple ramps up.

At first, when they say, "I love you," they're doing it in front of other people for show. But that first time the words come out of their mouths in private and they mean it? Like, really, really mean it? That moment will crack your readers' hearts open every single time.

"I Love You, No Really"

♦ SCENARIO ♦

Possible reasons your main protagonists are in a Fake Relationship: She needs a date for her ex's wedding; he's a celebrity (and infamous philanderer) who hires her to be his fake girlfriend to get the gossips off his back; she needs to relocate, fast, so she marries her friend in another kingdom. Whatever the reason, they've been carrying on this charade for a while and your protagonist needs to get something off her chest.

♦ BRAINSTORM ♦

Is it possible to fake something for so long that you can't tell the difference between fake and real anymore? Think about your protagonist's relationship history and describe a couple of the more significant romances she's had. How long has it been since she told someone "I love you" and meant it? Has she ever *truly* been in love? If not, why not?

♦ WRITE ♦

Write a scene where your protagonist says "I love you" to her fake love interest, who doesn't realize your protagonist means it. How many times must your protagonist say the words until the love interest gets what's going on? Does he share your protagonist's feelings? If so, does he say the words back or is he too thrown off by this unexpected revelation?

♦ OPTIONAL ELEMENTS TO INCLUDE ♦

- Stunned laughter.
- An awful moment of silence.
- The love interest isn't sure if he heard correctly.

Fantasy Twist

What if your protagonist is from another kingdom/land/world and English isn't her mother tongue? Maybe she says "I love you" in this other language first, to test the waters before she finds the courage to say it in a way her love interest will understand.

Callbacks

Look at every fake "I love you" these two characters say to each other. How can you differentiate this one, so your readers immediately know they are in new territory?

"You Thought That Was Real?"

◆ SCENARIO ◆

Their relationship started out fake . . . but at some point, things changed. Your protagonist knows it's real now, even though she hasn't verbalized the shift. When someone accuses her of faking it and she tells the truth—"It was fake until it got real"—her love interest contradicts her. She's horrified. How could she have gotten this so wrong?

◆ BRAINSTORM ◆

Why are they afraid to be real with each other? Think of a moment from their respective pasts where they were traumatized by love. How much power does the past hold over them? Does it impact them in any other ways?

◆ WRITE ◆

Your protagonist is shocked that her fake lover doesn't believe she really loves him. How dare he deny what she feels? Write the aftermath of this betrayal.

◆ OPTIONAL ELEMENTS TO INCLUDE ◆

- A moment of rage.
- A gentle plea to "take that back."
- A kiss denied.

Callbacks

Think about the moment they made this fake dating arrangement. Has your protagonist broken their original pact by developing feelings?

"I Didn't Know That about You"

◆ SCENARIO ◆

Your protagonist won't get her inheritance unless she's married, so she either marries a friend or pays an acquaintance to pose as her spouse. She suddenly finds herself spending all her time with this person and getting to know him in deeply intimate ways.

◆ BRAINSTORM ◆

Think about how different it is to be casual friends versus sharing a living space. Make a list of all the things you know about the people you live with that wouldn't come up in other relationships.

◆ WRITE ◆

Write a scene where your protagonist and her fake love interest are about to set out on a long journey. Come up with high-pressure stakes for their trip: They must destroy a cursed object; they must retrieve a long-lost magical weapon that once belonged to your protagonist's family; they must save your protagonist's sister, who was abducted by a roaming gang of vampires, etc. As they prepare to leave, your protagonist learns something shocking about her pretend partner.

◆ OPTIONAL ELEMENTS TO INCLUDE ◆

- Your protagonist is so stunned she doesn't even know how to reply.
- A false start: They set out on their journey, then must suddenly return home.
- A moment where one of your main characters rambles uncomfortably.

Fantasy Twist

Your protagonist doesn't completely trust her partner. She puts a spell on his luggage, making it sentient. Suddenly, she's learning all this man's baggage directly from his baggage.

Callbacks

Whatever your protagonist learns about her partner, make it something that will keep coming up over the course of their journey. (For example, she learns he's terrified of insects, and they have to sleep in the forest, where they keep encountering strange bugs.)

Quick Writes

Set a timer for 15 minutes and do not stop writing until the timer goes off. Do not edit, cross out, or censor yourself. Write down every thought that comes to you.

1. Your protagonist is terrified of her feelings. Write a scene where she breaks up with her fake partner because it isn't fake for her anymore. She worries it will never be real for him.

2. Your protagonist is in a fake marriage to gain access to a community or club that only accepts married people. Write a scene where someone accuses them of faking it and threatens to report them to authorities.

3. Write a scene where your protagonist discovers her fake partner has been pining for her since before they made their arrangement. Does she feel betrayed or excited?

4. Write a scene where your main couple decides to get intimate out of curiosity, just to see if that feels "fake" too.

5. Your protagonist is getting paid to be in this fake arrangement, but she's starting to feel shame about the money. Write a scene where she returns the money and tells her partner it isn't fake for her anymore.

Opposites Attract

*I*t happens all the time. You meet someone in the workplace or your personal life who rubs you the wrong way and you back off. Why waste time getting close when there's a personality conflict from the start? Here's one good reason: Opposites Attract. That irritating someone just might be the one you are meant to love forever.

When you're writing this scenario, make your opposites extreme. Put an alien and a human together, a comic and a curmudgeon, an overachiever and a slouch, a witch and a royal, an athlete and a klutz, a psychic and a scientist, a slob and a neatnik. You get the idea. The more your protagonist differs from her love interest, the more conflict you create. Make their journey into each other's arms surprising, agonizing, and exhilarating.

It will take some soul-searching for these characters to figure out what they want. How do they overcome the idea that they can never be compatible with someone so annoying? There will be battles and hijinks along the way, but they will eventually discover there's an invisible magnetic force at work here. Nothing can keep them apart.

" I Don't Feel Like Myself "

◆ SCENARIO ◆

Your protagonist is dating the kind of person she never imagined she'd like. They bicker—a lot. But under all the bluster, he's kind. He gives her flowers and does good deeds for strangers without taking credit. And the sex is mind-blowingly awesome.

◆ BRAINSTORM ◆

Your protagonist and her love interest had a physical connection before they got to know each other. Think about their favorite moves in the bedroom. What would readers be surprised to know about their carnal likes and dislikes? Try to shock yourself as you write.

◆ WRITE ◆

Write a scene where your protagonist goes on an epic rant about how wrong she and her love interest are for each other, but how much she likes and wants him anyway. Have her list all the reasons why this relationship shouldn't work. Then have her list all the reasons why it could work despite how she feels. She hates hating him—so she's decided this isn't how their love story has to play out.

◆ OPTIONAL ELEMENTS TO INCLUDE ◆

- The love interest tries to interrupt but she keeps talking.
- The love interest joins her rant, adding more reasons he's wrong for her.
- Onlookers crowd around to listen.

Fantasy Twist

What if this was an upstairs/downstairs love story that takes place in an enchanted castle? Think of all the crevices and secret spaces they might sneak off to when they need private spicy time.

Callbacks

Your protagonist might refer to earlier scenes between her and her love interest in her rant. Reveal how her impression of this person has evolved—from better to worse and back again.

"If You Think I'd Want to Be with You, You're Crazy"

◆ SCENARIO ◆

Your protagonist has feelings for someone who's wrong for her. That's what everyone says, at least. When she confesses her feelings to her crush anyway, he echoes her friends: "We're too different; it'll never work." Ouch. (That's why they're called crushes, right?) But then he throws her an emotional curveball . . .

◆ BRAINSTORM ◆

Get into the love interest's head. Is he telling the truth when he says he doesn't think they're a good match, or is he also facing pressure from outside forces? What if his friends are feeding him the same nonsense "it'll never work" line? What does he really think?

◆ WRITE ◆

Here's what the love interest suggests: "Let's hook up, but keep it secret from our friends." So, in public, they'll pretend to be enemies. In private, they'll follow their hearts. Write a scene where they get into a very public argument about interdimensional politics, or something equally polarizing. But the subtext of the entire fight is: I want you; I need you; I love you. Find a moment in the fight where they pivot and get personal.

Remember: They both mean the opposite of what they're saying. How can you have fun with that? Twist their words in clever ways that show your readers how conflicted they are.

◆ OPTIONAL ELEMENTS TO INCLUDE ◆

- They give each other nicknames.
- One of them is shouting so much they keep spitting.
- A grunt of frustration. Then another.

Fantasy Twist

What if you gave the power of Elemental Magic to the love interest? Play around with the idea that his emotions are reflected in the weather. He might say one thing in this fight, but the weather contradicts him—which gives your protagonist insight into his true feelings.

"Are We Really Doing This?"

◆ SCENARIO ◆

Your protagonist and her mismatched love interest are about to set off on a world-saving (cross your fingers) adventure. They already want to give up—how can they survive an epic journey together when they can barely agree on what to pack? Should they quit before they even start?

◆ BRAINSTORM ◆

What are their hesitations? Get into their heads and come up with a reason they're always at odds. You could delve into this by thinking about what they each want to bring with them on this trip. What does his bag of supplies say about him and vice versa?

◆ WRITE ◆

Write a scene where these two characters make a pact: No matter how hard the journey is, no matter how much they argue, they will have each other's backs.

◆ OPTIONAL ELEMENTS TO INCLUDE ◆

- An explosion.
- A whispered warning.
- An eye roll.

Fantasy Twist

Why exactly do these two characters think they can save the world? Is one of them a Level 16 paladin? Are they seasoned warriors? What if their supernatural powers only work when they're together? Even though they're opposites, find ways in which they complement each other.

Quick Writes

Set a timer for 15 minutes and do not stop writing until the timer goes off. Do not edit, cross out, or censor yourself. Write down every thought that comes to you.

1. Your protagonist is an eternal optimist; her lover is a perennial pessimist. Write a scene where she takes him to "the most beautiful thing I've ever seen." His heart melts.

2. Your protagonist embodies goodness (she might be a fairy or angel), and she's fallen for someone who embodies darkness (perhaps a demon). Write a scene where she is in grave danger, and he risks his life to save her.

3. Your protagonist is a neat freak; her partner is a slob. Write a scene where he does a striptease and lets his clothes fall wherever. She can't restrain herself from retrieving and folding them as they fall.

4. Your protagonist is a carefree creative type. Her love interest has a boring job and a boring life. Write a scene where she playfully kidnaps him for a date that goes off the rails. Whatever trouble they get into, it's anything but boring.

5. Your protagonist is gawky. Her lover is a Greek god. Write a scene where a stranger treats her like she's invisible and flirts with Mr. Greek God. Let your protagonist stand up for herself like never before.

Amnesia

Your protagonist wakes up one morning and doesn't know where or who she is. But even though her life's a blank page, the Amnesia trope gives you an opportunity for endless story possibilities. Here are just a few starting points:

Sweet: Your protagonist's spouse teaches her about the life she forgot. She gets to fall in love all over again.

Scary: A stranger pretends to be your protagonist's partner. How long until she realizes she's in mortal peril?

Curious: Someone tells your protagonist who she is, and she isn't very impressed with her life. Now she gets a second chance to do things differently.

Epic: Your protagonist is the only one with the power to save the kingdom/world/universe, but the key to the future is lost somewhere in her head. Will she remember in time?

Dramatic: Your protagonist is supposed to get married in a week. This marriage is destined to end a long-standing feud between two communities (werewolves and vamps, gods and monsters, humans and fae). But your protagonist doesn't want to marry someone she can't remember.

The question of whether your protagonist ever gets her memory back is not what matters most in an Amnesia story. It's all about the excitement of seeing her figure out who she was, who she is, and who she wants to be.

"I'm Not Who You Think I Am"

◆ SCENARIO ◆

Your protagonist is recovering from an accident that stole her memory. Thankfully, she has the best partner to help her in these difficult times. He's always there for her. He's perfect. What she doesn't remember is that things weren't always so rosy. Before she lost her memory, she wanted out. They were barreling toward a breakup. He sees her amnesia as a gift. A second chance.

◆ BRAINSTORM ◆

What were the couple's big issues in their pre-amnesia life? What did they fight about? Come up with enough backstory to understand why their relationship was destined for failure. Can they start over when their new relationship is founded on a lie?

◆ WRITE ◆

Write a scene where the love interest takes your protagonist on a date. It's romantic; it's sweet; it's thoughtful. But then the love interest says he has something scary to tell her. He feels guilty about the lies he's told. You decide how she reacts to his deception.

◆ OPTIONAL ELEMENTS TO INCLUDE ◆

- Your protagonist throws something across the room, and it shatters.
- Your protagonist doesn't believe her love interest at first—is this a prank?
- Your protagonist flashes on a moment from their past.

Fantasy Twist

What if your protagonist has a supernatural power she's forgotten about? It might awaken within her at moments of extreme emotion... like when she finds out her lover is a massive liar. What kind of power is it, and is it at full strength when it returns? Can she figure out how to control it?

Callbacks

The love interest says he's coming clean about their complicated past. But does he tell her the full truth? As he fills her in on memories she's forgotten, you decide what parts of these stories are true and if any of these "truths" are pure fabrication.

"If You Don't Stop Following Me, You're Going to Regret It"

◆ SCENARIO ◆

Your amnesiac protagonist has a messy breakup with her lover. She doesn't want to be with someone she can't remember. It feels like she's living someone else's life. He says she's making a mistake. She's sorry to hurt him—but this is the only decision that feels right. Will he respect her choice?

◆ BRAINSTORM ◆

If your protagonist has little flashes of memory, what might they look like? Instead of specifics, she can only see fractured pictures. Come up with five partial memories that might give her some clues about what her ex was like in the past. Remember to mix in the good and the bad.

◆ WRITE ◆

Write a scene where your protagonist realizes she's being followed. She doesn't know who it is or what they want—but someone is there. Is it her jilted ex or an enemy from her past? Whatever you decide, go for a thriller vibe as your protagonist finds herself in a situation where she senses danger, but amnesia keeps her from identifying her enemy.

◆ OPTIONAL ELEMENTS TO INCLUDE ◆

- Your protagonist sees something that isn't there.
- Your protagonist gets jostled by strangers in a crowd.
- A near-death experience.
- An act of transformation.

Fantasy Twist

What if your protagonist is part of the upper class, a member of high society? Maybe even royalty? How might this stalking scenario intensify if she lived someplace like a castle or an impenetrable fortress, and yet she still doesn't feel safe?

Callbacks

What might trigger memories for your protagonist? Are there any words, phrases, actions, or images that might send her hurtling back into the past? Does she know anyone who might be able to cast a "fall back" spell that sends her back in time to investigate her own life?

"Look What I Found in My Pocket"

◆ SCENARIO ◆

Your protagonist tries to piece together her lost past with the help of her new love interest. It's like putting together a puzzle, and she's enjoying the mystery. Your protagonist doesn't feel scared—since everything's a blank, it's exciting every time she learns something new. But then she's presented with a scary new piece of information.

◆ BRAINSTORM ◆

What are the skeletons in your protagonist's closet? Does she have any dark secrets? Think about things she might want to keep buried in her past, if only she could remember she doesn't *want* to remember them. What about her love interest? Does he have any dark secrets of his own? Or are his intentions good and pure? Explore both characters' past lives.

◆ WRITE ◆

Write a scene where your protagonist finds a big clue about who she used to be. This is the first time she feels any trepidation about her former life. This feels like a bad omen. What might this revelation portend?

Remember: Your protagonist has the tools to solve the mystery of who she is and where she came from. She must find the courage to dig deeper when she discovers something she'd rather not know.

◆ OPTIONAL ELEMENTS TO INCLUDE ◆

- Something broken.
- Something burned.
- Something rose red.

Fantasy Twist

Who could your protagonist turn to for help figuring out what this clue means? What if this discovery has the potential to send her (and her lover) on a journey to worlds they never even knew existed? Will they go?

Callbacks

What if your protagonist was hiding something from other people when she lost her memory? Even though she didn't lose her memory intentionally, she has effectively hidden her secret from herself. Would she be better off if she didn't learn the truth?

Quick Writes

Set a timer for 15 minutes and do not stop writing until the timer goes off. Do not edit, cross out, or censor yourself. Write down every thought that comes to you.

1. Write a scene where your protagonist finds an old diary hidden in her bedroom. As she reads, she unlocks a mystery from her past.

2. Your protagonist is The Chosen One. Before she lost her memory, she was getting ready to embark on a journey to defeat a great enemy. Now she's afraid to go. Write a scene where her lover, her mentor, and her best friend convince her she can do this.

3. Write a scene where your amnesiac protagonist gets into a harrowing accident and suddenly all her memories come rushing back.

4. Your protagonist's lover has lost his memory. Write a scene where she takes him to an important place from their past, hoping it might trigger a breakthrough.

5. Your protagonist is the victim of a curse. Write a scene where she makes the difficult decision to wipe her own memory clean—to give herself a fresh start.

Fish Out of Water

Take a character out of her comfort zone, put her in a place she's never been—figuratively or literally—and watch what happens. She will flail around like a Fish Out of Water. What better opportunity to introduce a love interest who exudes strength, stability, and self-assurance? Better yet, make it someone your protagonist wouldn't normally be attracted to. It's easier to take a risk on someone outside the ordinary when you're struggling to get your bearings in a new environment.

A Fish Out of Water romance might revolve around an alien creature who has landed in a small town where everything is foreign, but a certain someone helps her and it's love at first sight. Maybe the Fish Out of Water is a person from a large corporation who visits a small subsidiary where the hot CEO leads with a completely different set of values. Or your protagonist travels a great distance to claim an inheritance that draws her into a universe totally unlike her own.

Whatever the circumstances you set up, your character will be changed—in a good way—as she adapts to her new surroundings and falls in love. Lean into the humor that comes up as someone who has no clue where she's going arrives in a strange new place and tries to fit in. Make her awkward, adorable, irresistible. And have her face challenges that are ultimately resolved by heartwarming, inspiring revelations and relationships.

"I've Never Felt More Uncomfortable in My Entire Life"

◆ SCENARIO ◆

Your protagonist is not from this world. She's doing her best to fit in, but it feels like everything was designed to make her frustrated. She can't get used to the customs here, the language seems unusually complicated, and she keeps messing up and doing unacceptable things. But then she meets someone who makes her feel like it's okay not to fit in.

◆ BRAINSTORM ◆

Take five traditions, customs, or rules that people follow in the world of your story. Are there any equivalent traditions, customs, or rules in the world where your protagonist is from? Think of some of the ways these two worlds are similar—bridges the love interest might create for your protagonist to help her feel more comfortable here.

◆ WRITE ◆

Write a scene where your Fish-Out-of-Water protagonist has a meltdown. She's been trying so hard to assimilate, but she can't. Her love interest is incredibly patient as he lets her vent and listens without judging. He offers support without telling her what to do. He makes her feel heard and lets her know she's never a burden.

◆ OPTIONAL ELEMENTS TO INCLUDE ◆

- A moment of unexpected violence inflicted by a cruel world.
- Your protagonist stumbles over her words.
- A long, tight, comforting hug.

Fantasy Twist

What if your protagonist has an ability that ordinary people in this new world don't possess? Telepathy? Telekinesis? Precognition? Clairvoyance? Back home, there's nothing special about her power. Here, she's a freak.

Callbacks

Write a flashback scene to show how different your protagonist's life was in her own world. Show your readers her former status quo so they understand the culture shock she feels now.

"That's Not How It Works"

◆ SCENARIO ◆

Your protagonist told a big lie. She pretended to be qualified for a job she doesn't have a clue how to do. She figures she can learn on the fly. She'll just dive into the deep end and teach herself how to swim. But as soon as she starts her new job, it quickly becomes clear this won't be as easy as she thought.

◆ BRAINSTORM ◆

What line of work is your protagonist trying to Trojan Horse herself into? Is it a job you know a lot about, or do you feel equally unqualified? Do some research right now.

◆ WRITE ◆

Write a scene where a coworker accuses your protagonist of not knowing what she's talking about. Is this coworker antagonistic? Flirtatious? As he shows your protagonist the ropes, they get to know each other in unexpected ways. Your protagonist doesn't know what she's doing, but she knows *who* she's doing. Hopefully soon.

◆ OPTIONAL ELEMENTS TO INCLUDE ◆

- ♦ A casual touch.
- ♦ A shared treat.
- ♦ The coworker stretches, exposing impressive abs.

Fantasy Twist

What line of work is your protagonist trying to break into? Create a job specific to your world. It could be anything from Time Travel Guide to Spell Binding to Werewolf Fashion. Be creative.

"I Don't Even Know Who I Am Anymore"

◆ SCENARIO ◆

Your protagonist can separate her life into two eras: before and after. Maybe she moved to a faraway place where she didn't fit in. Maybe she pivoted from one career to another and there was a wild learning curve. Whatever her new situation is, her alienated feelings are fading.

◆ BRAINSTORM ◆

Think about the new language your protagonist must learn to navigate this universe. Are there words or phrases she knows now that would have flummoxed her before? Make a glossary of terms connected to your protagonist's new life.

◆ WRITE ◆

Write a scene where your protagonist goes on a first date with someone in her new world. She is beginning to thrive here, and as a result she shows a new confidence on this date. Who cares if her date likes her or not—she's surprised by how much more she likes herself.

Remember: It wasn't that long ago that your protagonist didn't fit in here. Do we get any glimpses of her former, insecure self? How far removed is she from the person she used to be?

◆ OPTIONAL ELEMENTS TO INCLUDE ◆

- Your protagonist's confidence is contagious—literally.
- Your protagonist begins to glow.
- Your protagonist challenges her date to do something dangerous.

Fantasy Twist

What if there's a supernatural reason your protagonist has begun to fit in so well? Is it possible she's gotten a little help from a magical friend? Or perhaps a spell has fortified her courage?

Callbacks

Have your protagonist open up to her date about something she didn't like about her previous life. Have her talk about all the reasons she didn't like it. Being vulnerable about her past will help her gain confidence about her future.

Quick Writes

Set a timer for 15 minutes and do not stop writing until the timer goes off. Do not edit, cross out, or censor yourself. Write down every thought that comes to you.

1. Your protagonist elopes with a foreign prince. Write a scene where she's hounded by people begging for aid. Your protagonist wants to help everyone. She's in over her head.

2. Write a scene where your protagonist discovers an alien baby on her front doorstep. She has no idea how to take care of this creature.

3. Your wealthy, spoiled protagonist has been abducted by mercenaries from another planet. Write a scene where she confesses her love to the guard who brings her food.

4. Your protagonist recently had plastic surgery to implant gills (or wings) to be closer to the gilled (or winged) love of her life. Write a scene where she finds out his family still doesn't approve.

5. Your protagonist comes from wealth, but her kingdom has been vanquished. Write a scene where she tries to start over but realizes she doesn't know how to do anything.

THE BET

When someone who thinks they're immune to love places The Bet, there's more at risk than money. This is a wicked game of hearts that takes twists and turns before the truth comes out.

Here's how The Bet might work:

A friend bets your protagonist she can't attract the interest of someone who's out of her league. Maybe it's her boss, or the King of the Damned (hello, vampire royalty!), or a powerful elected official. Whatever makes him unattainable doesn't matter because your protagonist has enough ego to believe this person can't resist her. So, hell yes, it's on.

The stakes are usually monetary. For example: If your protagonist wins, she gets an all-expenses-paid trip to the exotic world of her choice. If she loses, she pays for her friend's trip.

But then genuine feelings develop between your deceitful protagonist and her unwitting love interest. The stakes of The Bet are now less important than this person who might be The One.

But before she can come clean, the love interest finds out and all bets are off. The problem is, despite all the hurt and pain, these characters are genuinely in love.

The final twist becomes the repair work they need to do so they can bet on a future together—without secrets.

"I Knew There Was Something Wrong with You"

◆ SCENARIO ◆

Your protagonist doesn't know about The Bet her new love interest has with his friends. (Make it a shameful bet—something casually mean-spirited.) She's been on a few dates with this guy now, and she's having fun getting to know him. Tonight, they will get to know each other more deeply. She will open up about things she's never told another living soul. But she fully trusts him, so she thinks it's going to be okay.

◆ BRAINSTORM ◆

Think like your protagonist. Imagine she's looking back at her life and critiquing what she sees. What are the biggest mistakes she's ever made? What are her greatest regrets? What does she wish she could get a second chance at? Make a list of her worst moments. Her most unforgivable deeds. What cruelties has she inflicted upon loved ones?

◆ WRITE ◆

Write a playful, flirtatious scene where these two characters decide to share all their faults. It's your protagonist's idea. She thinks it'll bring them closer. Maybe they make it a game: Whoever can top the other one with "the worst thing you've ever done" must pay for dinner.

Remember: As far as they go in tonight's game, the love interest holds one thing back: He doesn't mention The Bet your protagonist is unwittingly playing a part in. He knows that's a bridge too far. Which is why it's dangerous to get so invested in this.

◆ OPTIONAL ELEMENTS TO INCLUDE ◆

- A public display of affection.
- A giggling fit.
- They get kicked out of a restaurant because they've stayed until after closing.

Fantasy Twist

If your characters are supernatural, you might get away with some of their past actions being truly heinous. Your protagonist shows her trust by laying herself bare. Who cares if she did a despicable thing in her youth? She feels comfortable admitting anything to this person because she's certain he's trustworthy. If only she knew what was coming...

"I'm a Terrible Loser"

◆ SCENARIO ◆

Your protagonist made The Bet with her friends—something like "whoever finds the dumbest boyfriend gets treated to a spa day" or "whoever gets a guy to buy you the most expensive gift gets to pick what galaxy we go to for our next girls' trip." Whatever the stakes, your protagonist quickly begins to regret The Bet. She likes the guy she asks out, and now she's trapped in a lie. She wants to call the whole thing off with her friends so she can date this guy for real.

◆ BRAINSTORM ◆

Think about the dynamics in this friend group. Who is the worst loser? Who is the most competitive? And who came up with the idea for The Bet in the first place?

◆ WRITE ◆

Write a scene where your protagonist tries to cancel The Bet, but her friends won't let her. They don't think it's fair to back out now. Maybe one of them threatens to expose your friend to her lover if she doesn't see The Bet through all the way to the end.

Remember: There's a lot going on here. Your protagonist may not only have to face the loss of her lover at the end of all of this, but the loss of The Bet itself. Think about what she values more: her new love or her pride. The answer would be easy if she weren't so competitive.

◆ OPTIONAL ELEMENTS TO INCLUDE ◆

- ◆ A slap in the face.
- ◆ Raised stakes.
- ◆ A repeated plea.

Fantasy Twist

What if The Bet had real-world consequences? Think about what communities the love interest is part of. If/when he finds himself shamed and embarrassed, what might other people (or creatures) in his community do to get revenge?

Callbacks

Your protagonist was eager to participate in The Bet when the idea initially came up. Have her friends use her own words against her in this scene.

"Can We Go Back to the Beginning?"

◆ SCENARIO ◆

Your protagonist was involved in The Bet. Either she came up with the idea or she was a victim; it doesn't matter. At this point in your story, The Bet is over, and everyone knows the truth. Your protagonist and her love interest have broken up. They hate being apart, but can they ever trust each other again?

◆ BRAINSTORM ◆

Think about how traumatic it would be to discover your relationship was built on a lie. Being a victim of The Bet is worse than just falling for a normal lie, isn't it? How would you personally feel if you were in this situation? Do some freewriting about your own possible reactions and then give your specific emotions to your protagonist or the love interest (depending on which one was the victim of The Bet).

◆ WRITE ◆

Write a scene where the couple decides to start over because there's no way to move on from where they currently stand. They will pretend none of this happened and start from square one.

◆ OPTIONAL ELEMENTS TO INCLUDE ◆

- A repeated line of dialogue.
- A renewed sense of hope.
- A kiss that feels different from last time.

Fantasy Twist

What if they literally start over by traveling back in time to when they met—or even earlier, to a moment before The Bet? Would it be possible for them to have a real chance at a fresh start?

Callbacks

When your protagonist and love interest first met, what were they wearing? Think about how The Bet changes the way your protagonist looks at a certain item of clothing or jewelry. Does she make a choice not to wear something again because it reminds her of betrayal and deceit?

Quick Writes

Set a timer for 15 minutes and do not stop writing until the timer goes off. Do not edit, cross out, or censor yourself. Write down every thought that comes to you.

1. Write a scene where your protagonist discovers that her love interest asked her out as part of The Bet—and in her anger, she destroys an entire city.

2. Write a scene where the love interest confesses to your protagonist that he started dating her as part of The Bet, then she turns the tables on him and reveals she's been dating him because of a bet too.

3. Write a scene where your protagonist discovers her entire relationship is being televised or streamed as part of a massive underground bet that millions of people are involved in.

4. Write a scene where your protagonist discovers she's part of The Bet and instead of getting upset, she's flattered. Think of this as a foreplay scene.

5. Write a scene where your protagonist confesses that she started dating her love interest as part of The Bet, and he confesses that he's known the entire time.

Just Friends

Forever friends tend to be clueless about their romantic potential. They love each other but—OMG—they could never make love with each other. *No thank you*, they agree. (Without ever talking about it.) *We are Just Friends*, they think, *and that's how it's always going to be.*

"Clueless" is the operative word here. One day, something happens that sends them into each other's arms for a supportive hug. Hmmm. This feels good. They linger . . . and suddenly their lips lock. Your protagonist pulls away and talks about something inane—anything to distract her from The Kiss.

Both friends are shocked by how they feel. But there's an obstacle that can't be overcome. One is dating the other's sibling or maybe one is engaged. Or they just can't believe they could ever be more than BFFs. So, they decide to be clear with each other: This can never happen again.

But now they know. And they won't be able to deny their romantic feelings for each other much longer. Maybe they need a nudge from someone who can speak to them in a dream or place a spell on them—anything to help them realize they were never meant to be Just Friends.

"Promise Me We'll Never Change"

◆ SCENARIO ◆

Your main characters wonder what it might be like to be with each other, but they're currently dating other people. They've never wanted to mess up their great friendship. Besides, they're with other people, remember? Then something happens that threatens this delicate balance.

◆ BRAINSTORM ◆

Make a list of qualities they like about each other that their respective partners don't have. Even though the people they're dating might be wonderful, both lack something your two protagonists want or need. Figure out the various pros and cons of each relationship.

◆ WRITE ◆

Your main protagonists accidentally kiss. It's consensual yet unexpected. Both admit: That was a good kiss. Another thing they agree on: They can never do that again. Too many people would get hurt. Write a scene where they negotiate how to salvage their friendship while not succumbing to their mutual desires.

◆ OPTIONAL ELEMENTS TO INCLUDE ◆

- An enticing scent or pheromone.
- Thoughts of the kiss run on a loop through one of their heads. The other is startled to discover they can hear their friend's thoughts.
- A sudden goodbye.

Fantasy Twist

What if your story is set in ancient times? Your characters might live in a small village or a medieval city. Think about where this kiss might happen. In the stables while caring for their equine companions? While taking cover as dragons attack their home from above? How might these settings impact how you handle the aftermath of The Kiss That Shall Not Be Named?

Callbacks

What if they come up with a code word for "kiss" so they can talk about this moment later, in mixed company, without anyone else knowing what they're discussing? Think about their motivations: Why do they feel the need to develop the code word? Are outside forces working against them?

"I Can't Believe You Did Me Dirty Like That"

◆ SCENARIO ◆

Your protagonist hooked up with this friend once. It was amazing, but there was one problem: The guy was dating someone she's close to—her sister, her best friend, or even her *mom*. (The mom might be a dark choice, but why not?) They agreed to remain friends and never mention this to anyone. Unfortunately, there appears to be a law of nature that says secrets must come out.

◆ BRAINSTORM ◆

Think about how often your protagonist and her "just friend" encounter each other. Quickly sketch out three of their most awkward encounters.

◆ WRITE ◆

Write a scene where your protagonist is confronted by her sister, best friend, or mom. They suspect something happened and demand answers. They're more hurt than angry, making this harder. Decide whether your protagonist admits the truth or lies.

Remember: This person who's confronting your protagonist has known her a long time. They can tell when your protagonist is lying.

◆ OPTIONAL ELEMENTS TO INCLUDE ◆

- One of them needs a drink.
- A bitter truth.
- Uncomfortable laughter.

Callbacks

Your protagonist knows too much about her "friend." For example, details about his body. What if one of those forbidden bits of information comes out in this scene?

"I've Got Your Back"

◆ SCENARIO ◆

Friend A has been married forever. Friend B goes from lover to lover, never settling down. These two friends have been through wars together. They've seen kingdoms fall. They've survived plagues. They've grown old together, but separately. They love each other, but they'll never admit it.

◆ BRAINSTORM ◆

How many times have they almost taken their relationship to the next level? Have they ever talked about these near misses? What would their lives look like if they allowed themselves to move past friendship?

◆ WRITE ◆

Write a scene where one of these characters is dying and they finally confess their love. Is it too little, too late? Or do they have one last epic adventure in them?

Remember: One of these characters is married. What happens to their spouse now that your main characters are together? How long has the spouse known about their feelings?

◆ OPTIONAL ELEMENTS TO INCLUDE ◆

- An old photograph, kept folded away.
- Entwined fingers.
- A story repeated, with new context.

Fantasy Twist

Is there a way for them to go back to a time and place where they might get a second chance? What would they give up if it meant they could be More Than Friends, for once?

Quick Writes

Set a timer for 15 minutes and do not stop writing until the timer goes off. Do not edit, cross out, or censor yourself. Write down every thought that comes to you.

1. Write a scene where two friends give each other relationship advice while struggling not to touch each other.

2. Write a scene where two friends feverishly admit their feelings for each other, in front of their respective spouses, and tragedy immediately strikes. Did they make the gods mad?

3. Write a scene where your protagonist confesses her feelings for her best friend's betrothed to a priest or chaplain while a snake (literal or figurative) eavesdrops.

4. Write a scene where your protagonist seeks help from an old crone, who promises to drain the love from your protagonist's heart. No more pining for an unattainable friend.

5. Write a scene where your protagonist and her friend make a "we'll get married if we're single at forty" pact. They sign an agreement to make it official. One of them has cold feet and doesn't realize the pact is binding—in a you'll-be-asleep-for-one-thousand-years-if-you-break-it kind of way. Now what?

Secret Royalty

People usually want to be loved for who they are rather than what they have, right? Your readers will be sympathetic toward a protagonist who hides something as big as Secret Royalty. They tried to embrace their birthright, but the crown never really fit.

Off-the-charts chemistry between the Royal and the Commoner drives this kind of romantasy, but the heart of these stories lies in your protagonist's discovery of something to live for that has nothing to do with wealth, fame, tradition, or power. And seeing how gobsmacked her love interest is when her true identity is revealed. The love interest might be hurt by the deceit, but ultimately love conquers all: The Royal gets to be real, and the Commoner gets to be royal.

But wait. Let's try this again. What if your protagonist is a royal but doesn't know it? She was raised away from the castle to learn how the people of the kingdom live. Meanwhile, she falls in love. Your supporting characters might use magical powers to protect the big secret and prevent this match from interfering with the future monarch's path to royal life. But the secret is destined to come out. Even though truth throws your protagonist and her love interest into a tailspin, their love is strong enough to overcome anything. How they take charge of their own fate is the fun part. Just make sure you give your readers a fairy-tale ending, even if your lovers never move into the castle.

"If Anyone Finds Out, I'm Ruined"

◆ SCENARIO ◆

Your protagonist is in the middle of a whirlwind new romance. Things are progressing in all the right ways. But sometimes she suspects he's holding back. She senses there's something he isn't being completely honest about. Is there something wrong with Mr. Right?

◆ BRAINSTORM ◆

Your protagonist's love interest is Secret Royalty. Think about why he's hiding from his family. Does anyone know where he is? Are they looking for him? What are the consequences of denying his birthright?

◆ WRITE ◆

Write a scene where your protagonist confronts her lover after catching him in a lie. He admits he's been lying, but not about what she thinks. Let his royal revelation be so shocking that she faints. When she comes to, he makes her promise to keep it secret, but can she? She loves him, but is this too much baggage?

◆ OPTIONAL ELEMENTS TO INCLUDE ◆

- He produces proof of his identity: an item with a royal insignia.
- She has a panic attack when she learns his origin story.
- She admits to fantasies of being royal herself.

Fantasy Twist

What if the royal refugee is secretly being watched? Perhaps a raven, a wolf, or another mystical creature is keeping tabs on him and reporting to his parents back at the castle.

Callbacks

The love interest is pretending to be a civilian, but when you've spent your whole life as part of the royal family, some affectations are bound to break through. What clues can you plant that might tip off your protagonist? Does he always try to be the first one through a doorway? Does he have a certain way of handling a knife and fork? Is he embarrassed by public affection?

"Are You Telling Me What I Think You're Telling Me?"

◆ SCENARIO ◆

Your protagonist is living two lives. By day, she serves the kingdom as part of the royal family. At sundown, she sneaks out for wild fun. One night, she meets someone incredibly ordinary who she really likes. Someone who has no idea who she is.

◆ BRAINSTORM ◆

Imagine how it would feel if every stranger had an opinion about your family. Do some freewriting in your protagonist's voice, digging into her complicated feelings about her upbringing and her family. What does she love most about her life and what does she hate?

◆ WRITE ◆

Write a scene where your protagonist "comes out" as royal to her new lover, who had absolutely no idea. Give the lover an extreme reaction. (Shock? Joy? Anger? Envy? You decide.)

◆ OPTIONAL ELEMENTS TO INCLUDE ◆

- A carafe of wine.
- The love interest doesn't believe her at first.
- Your protagonist tries to backtrack after telling her secret.

Fantasy Twist

What if the love interest comes from a family who holds an ancient grudge against the royals? Those ancestors, blessed with eternal youth, could still be a threat.

"I Only Want to Be the Queen of Your Heart"

◆ SCENARIO ◆

Your protagonist has been running away from her destiny. She's traversed cities, countries, oceans, possibly even worlds. Her family wanted too much, so she left. But it is time to step up. Her kingdom is in danger. They need her.

◆ BRAINSTORM ◆

Think about the many ways her kingdom might be failing. How bad have things gotten in your protagonist's absence? Is her family still alive? What bloody legacy awaits her if she decides to go back?

◆ WRITE ◆

Write a scene where your protagonist's lover discovers her secret and tries to convince her to accept her destiny. She fights it, listing all the reasons she can't go home. A part of her knows her lover is right, but she's not ready to accept it. Returning home means becoming Queen, which makes her responsible for saving her people. Can she become the heroine they need her to be? Her lover thinks so.

◆ OPTIONAL ELEMENTS TO INCLUDE ◆

- A message or warning comes to your protagonist in a dream.
- The lover is overcome with emotion.
- Your protagonist gets overwhelmed and shuts down.

Callbacks

Your protagonist once made an oath to her kingdom. Her lover might repeat this oath to her now, to help her see where her duty lies.

Quick Writes

Set a timer for 15 minutes and do not stop writing until the timer goes off. Do not edit, cross out, or censor yourself. Write down every thought that comes to you.

1. Your protagonist does not know she's a princess. Write a scene where she confronts the dashing man who has been following her for weeks (who was secretly sent from another kingdom in a faraway galaxy to make sure she stays out of trouble).

2. Your protagonist has forsaken her royal heritage to live a normal life. Write a scene where an unstable stranger recognizes her, but she is whisked away to safety by a sweet, normal guy.

3. Write a morning-after scene where your protagonist snoops through her new lover's belongings and discovers an ancient talisman with the royal insignia on it.

4. Write a scene where your main couple is interrupted in flagrante delicto by a henchman who has come to retrieve your protagonist. She is needed to break a royal curse. Her stunned lover had no idea who she was—and demands to tag along.

5. Write a scene where your protagonist explains to her lover why she's in hiding. If her royal parents knew her whereabouts, they would kill her.

Found Family

With blood relatives, you're lucky if you win the birth lottery and land in a loving, well-adjusted family. Honestly, it's a crap shoot. Then there's Found Family—the one you choose. You form a special bond with these people. Spending time with them is never an obligation. It's always a choice, and they know it. They see and love you as you are, and they make your life richer in ways no one else can.

When you're writing a Found Family story, you get to create a personal army for your protagonist. These people will protect her no matter what. They will root for her relationship to thrive, and if her love interest does her dirty, they will be there to help her pick up the pieces.

While a Found Family story will have a romance at its core, the love your protagonist shares with these characters is also a romance in and of itself. Build these relationships with care. Your readers will root for good things to happen for them too.

And remember, your protagonist can choose anyone for her Found Family. This is a chance to create a cast of characters who are diverse in more ways than one. They can come from different communities, as well as different species or fantasy worlds. Broaden your protagonist's horizons.

"They Never Knew Me Like You Know Me"

◆ SCENARIO ◆

Your protagonist has fallen in with a motley crew of misfits, artists, and underground activists. They take care of each other. Several nights a week they gather for huge potluck dinners that often go for hours, with drinking, dancing, and stories. So many stories.

◆ BRAINSTORM ◆

Think of three reasons your protagonist is no longer in touch with her blood relatives. What was the final straw that caused her to cut off contact? What parts of these stories might she share with others, and what parts might be too raw and emotional to reveal?

◆ WRITE ◆

Write a scene where your protagonist and a few of her Found Family members trauma-bond, telling each other about the worst parts of their childhood. But instead of getting depressed, they find it uplifting to know they aren't the only ones with awful childhoods. At one point, have your protagonist break away from the group for a one-on-one with someone she's particularly intrigued by. Their connection runs deeper . . .

Remember: These characters are getting to know each other, so they have a lot to cover. They speak freely because they know they aren't being judged in the ways they would be with their blood relatives.

◆ OPTIONAL ELEMENTS TO INCLUDE ◆

- Two characters discover they're both from the same faraway place.
- Your protagonist feels a maternal connection with someone in the group.
- Your protagonist and her love interest play footsie under the table.

Fantasy Twist

What if the water these characters imbibe at dinner is a magic potion that causes them to overshare without shame? Is there such a thing as revealing too much in a situation like this? Who goes too far?

"I Didn't Know Life Could Be So Good"

◆ SCENARIO ◆

Your protagonist didn't just have a bad childhood. She had the kind of childhood nightmares are made of. The members of her Found Family know that any mention of your protagonist's past is verboten. This is how your protagonist sees it: She has no past, only a present and a future.

◆ BRAINSTORM ◆

Even if you don't get explicit about the horrors of your protagonist's past, it will help to know some of what she's trying to forget. Quickly jot down five moments your protagonist wants to scrub from her memory. Pretend you're her therapist taking notes on these incidents, without judgment or emotion. Just the facts.

◆ WRITE ◆

Write a scene where your protagonist has an emotional breakthrough with her Found Family: She never thought she would have a family or friends like this. She never saw this future for herself. The truth is, she never thought she'd live long enough to feel this kind of joy. It's overwhelming. Give your protagonist a heartfelt speech about how lucky she is. Alternately, you could make this a private moment with just your protagonist and her love interest.

◆ OPTIONAL ELEMENTS TO INCLUDE ◆

- An impromptu dance party, with a group sing-along.
- A moment of anxiety, where your protagonist gets shaky.
- A good hug.

Fantasy Twist

What if your protagonist has a magical journal that talks back to her? Kind of like Siri, but not. A book she physically writes in that can speak and feel and help her work through her emotions. What sorts of things would it say?

Callbacks

Your protagonist might hint at moments from her past, but don't let her go too deep into her trauma. This isn't the time for that. She only gives a glimpse, a hint. Make it feel like her past is fading, or her bad memories are finally being replaced with good ones.

❝ Don't Worry, I've Got You ❞

◆ SCENARIO ◆

Your protagonist is used to doing the hard stuff alone. No one's ever had her back. Over the years, she's built walls up around her. She protects herself when no one else will.

◆ BRAINSTORM ◆

People with healthy families have support! Make a list of things a kid normally has help with. Now imagine your protagonist doing each of these activities alone.

◆ WRITE ◆

Write a scene where your protagonist is about to try something she's afraid to do. As she heads out, one member of her Found Family says they're coming too. Then another joins. And another. Your protagonist suddenly sees how fortunate she is.

◆ OPTIONAL ELEMENTS TO INCLUDE ◆

- A homemade gift.
- Laughing through tears.
- Someone takes your protagonist's hand when she falters.

Fantasy Twist

What if this is bigger than just an outing or a chore? What if your protagonist is setting out on an epic journey to repair a broken world she left behind thousands of years ago? And now she has her own personal crew.

Callbacks

Maybe your protagonist had a quiet moment with her love interest earlier, where he promised to join her on this dangerous mission. She assumed he was being nice but wouldn't come. She's wrong.

Quick Writes

Set a timer for 15 minutes and do not stop writing until the timer goes off. Do not edit, cross out, or censor yourself. Write down every thought that comes to you.

1. Your protagonist is a shifter. Write a scene where she admits to her new group of friends that they're the only people who've ever made her feel comfortable being her true self.

2. Your protagonist has a special power that has always ostracized her. An attractive stranger approaches her and says, "You are not alone." Write a scene where this stranger takes her to meet a group of others with this same power.

3. Write a dinner/feast scene, where your protagonist and her Found Family share stories about their childhood and bond over their various traumas. Together, they're stronger.

4. Write a scene where your protagonist welcomes someone new into her Found Family and promises she will be this person's new mother/sister/identifier-of-your-choice.

5. Your protagonist lost a battle and nearly died. She wakes to find strangers nursing her back to health. Write a scene where she meets everyone, including an intriguing and handsome guy who's also recovering from intense wounds.

Touch Her and Die

The protagonist of your story might be a knight in shining armor, a sorcerer, a dragon tamer, the ruler of a vast medieval kingdom, or even an ordinary citizen of this world or another. Whoever he is, there will be hell to pay if anyone messes with his lover. When your hero says, "Touch Her and Die," he doesn't just mean, "Leave her alone or I'll kill you." He means, "I will fight to the death if that's what it takes to protect the love of my life."

Don't we all secretly hope for a special someone willing to sacrifice everything just to keep us safe?

This trope is about true love fueled by extreme emotions and actions. Put a spotlight on the outrageous things larger-than-life heroes will do in the name of love.

This trope works best when your protagonist's love interest is an equally strong character—someone courageous and caring who has earned every good thing that has ever come her way. Show us why this person is so deserving of your protagonist's devotion. Feel free to make the love interest the hero/protector of your story. Regardless of who is doing the saving, this is a love story on steroids, so go for a grand finale. Once the threat has been conquered, bring your lovers together in a way that sets off fireworks on an intergalactic scale.

One more thing: Don't feel constrained when it comes to the gender of your protagonist in these stories: Your hero can be him, her, or they, and this trope could just as easily be called "Touch Him and Die" as "Touch Her and Die." Just tell a great story.

"You Don't Want to Test Me"

◆ SCENARIO ◆

Your protagonist has suffered several losses. She's tired of feeling like she can't take care of herself and her loved ones, so she's secretly been studying spell craft, potions, and curses. She's prepared to do damage, if necessary, to protect someone she loves—particularly that special someone in her life. Then she discovers she's not the only hero in her home. Her lover is making a superhero effort to physically strengthen himself in order to be ready to protect her.

◆ BRAINSTORM ◆

Come up with three curses or potions (or other prepared items/magic) your protagonist has expertly honed. What ingredients or words does she need? And is there any possibility these curses or potions might backfire? What are the potential side effects?

◆ WRITE ◆

Write a scene where your protagonist overhears her lover standing up for her and threatening one of her enemies. What sorts of things does he say, and does he have the power to back up those words? She's been getting ready to do this on her own, but her lover stepped in and did it for her. Knowing that she's not alone in this makes her heart burst.

Remember: Your protagonist didn't know her lover had this in him. Think about how this act of defense changes how your protagonist sees him and makes their bond stronger. It's rare in a couple, but aren't two heroes better than one?

◆ OPTIONAL ELEMENTS TO INCLUDE ◆

- ◆ Wild, passionate, post-confrontation sex.
- ◆ Your protagonist curses her enemy during her lover's confrontation.
- ◆ A strange weather phenomenon shifts the course of events.

Fantasy Twist

Your protagonist has been studying dark magic. What if she's stronger than she realizes? What if her anger has begun to manifest itself in the form of roots or vines growing around her home? What if these vines have thorns that could be lethal if touched?

"I've Eaten Bigger Men for Breakfast"

◆ SCENARIO ◆

People always underestimate your protagonist. But she's never been a damsel in distress. If anything, she's the one causing distress. There's someone in her life—it could be her lover, or a family member, or her best friend—who's in trouble. They tried to deal with this problem on their own, but it has only gotten worse. Finally, your protagonist asks them, "What's wrong?"

◆ BRAINSTORM ◆

How many fights has your protagonist gotten into? Does she have a weapon of choice? Think about her reputation and what potential opponents might think when they realize they're about to face her mano a mano.

◆ WRITE ◆

Write a scene where your protagonist stands up for her love interest. It starts with an ultimatum. But it quickly devolves into a massive, crazy, wild physical battle. Blood is shed! Property is destroyed! Your protagonist demonstrates inhuman strength. Her opponent is formidable too. Keep the suspense up as their fight ebbs and flows.

Remember: Fights can be boring when it's obvious who's going to win from the start. Make sure there are moments when it looks like this might not go the right way for your protagonist. If there was an official scorekeeper, both fighters would rack up points.

◆ OPTIONAL ELEMENTS TO INCLUDE ◆

- A harrowing sword fight.
- In the midst of battle, your characters tumble over the side of a cliff.
- Your protagonist gives her opponent a chance to give up.

Fantasy Twist

Does your protagonist have any secret weapons up her sleeve (either figuratively or literally)? Think of a fantastical surprise she might drop in the middle of this battle.

"You'd Really Do That for Me?"

◆ SCENARIO ◆

Your protagonist is in danger. She's being stalked by an ex, or her vindictive parents are trying to force her to come back to run the family business, or her former coven wants to burn her at the stake for leaving their fold. Whatever the situation, she's on the run. And she's tired of running.

◆ BRAINSTORM ◆

Is it possible for "fighting" to be someone's love language? What if that's how your protagonist's love interest expresses his feelings? Think about his various skill sets. How fearsome is he in battle? What forms of combat is he versed in? Does he have supernatural powers? How many physical fights has he been in? What percentage of fights does he win?

◆ WRITE ◆

Write a scene where the love interest tells your protagonist she doesn't have to run anymore. He will protect her. Does she know how he plans to do this? Does he want her to know? Regardless, she is overwhelmed by the idea of letting her guard down. She didn't know it would ever be possible to feel safe again—until she met him.

◆ OPTIONAL ELEMENTS TO INCLUDE ◆

- A playful "fight" between your protagonist and love interest that moves to the bedroom.
- An unexpected gift.
- A serious vow.

Fantasy Twist

Create a ticking clock by adding an element of disaster on the horizon. What if an asteroid is on the way, or their planet is being consumed by a black hole, or their city is in the middle of a barbaric coup? How do these big-picture events color the "smaller" events of your story?

Callbacks

What if the love interest reveals he's already begun protecting your protagonist without her knowledge? He tells her about a fight that your readers have already seen.

Quick Writes

Set a timer for 15 minutes and do not stop writing until the timer goes off. Do not edit, cross out, or censor yourself. Write down every thought that comes to you.

1. Your protagonist escaped a cult or a coven when she was younger. They have been sending her messages, beckoning her to return. Write a scene where her lover finds these messages and asks about her past. Her lover is furious and wants to protect her.

2. Your protagonist discovers her lover is being stalked by an ex. Write a scene where she shows up at the ex's home to convince them to back down, once and for all.

3. Write a scene where your protagonist finds out her lover has been issuing "Touch Her and Die" messages to many people in her life. She's upset that he thinks she can't protect herself.

4. Write a scene where an alien bodyguard confronts your protagonist's love interest about an old debt. Your protagonist stands up for her lover and repays his debt herself.

5. Your protagonist finds out a stranger defended her honor to her greatest enemy. Write a scene where she confronts the stranger, asking, "Who are you and why did you stand up for me?"

STRANDED

*I*magine you're stranded on a deserted island, or you're lost in the woods, or your aircraft crashed in the dunes of a sweltering planet. It sounds scary, difficult, terrible. Now imagine you aren't alone in this situation. You're with someone you find incredibly attractive, who's amazing in bed, and has survival skills you lack. That changes things, doesn't it?

Stranded stories can be especially fun to tell when you're writing romantasy because you get to create a unique world where your characters battle to survive. Think about the obstacles you can embed into the fabric of this universe. What creatures might they encounter? How extreme is the weather? What is the terrain like? What about the flora and fauna? What unknown dangers lurk where your protagonists might least expect them?

Stranded stories aren't about being lost—they're about the journey your protagonist goes through to be found. In this case, literally. But emotionally too. She wouldn't survive alone. By the end of your story, your protagonist and her love interest have earned their Happily Ever After because they got here together.

"I Could Kill You Right Now"

◆ SCENARIO ◆

Your protagonist and her love interest have fallen into a trap. It might be a deep hole, or a booby-trapped basement, or a human-sized garbage disposal—you decide. They're in danger. But as they spitball escape plans, neither one is listening to the other. Your protagonist is nearing the end of her (metaphorical) rope. But maybe there's a (literal) lifeline she's about to discover.

◆ BRAINSTORM ◆

If you were in this situation, how would you get out? Identify the pros and cons of several possible plans. Think about the specifics of the world your characters are in. Is there anything about the material the trap is made of, or the terrain the hole was dug into, that makes getting out more difficult? Are your characters alone in the trap, or is someone, or something, in there with them?

◆ WRITE ◆

Write a scene where these two characters get into a fight about how to save themselves. When your protagonist realizes her love interest isn't listening, she stops helping him. If they can't work together, they might as well die! Keep raising the stakes as their argument goes on—the longer they're down here, the less likely they are to get out.

◆ OPTIONAL ELEMENTS TO INCLUDE ◆

- One of them sprains an ankle.
- A moment where they're both out of breath.
- The walls begin to cave in.

Fantasy Twist

Imagine there's a creature in this trap with them. Is it poisonous? Rabid? Hungry? Have they ever encountered a creature like this before? Can they use the creature to help them get out?

Callbacks

Is there a skill you can plant earlier in your story that they can use here? For example, maybe one of them is a great climber. Or is there a tool you could establish earlier, perhaps in a backpack, that would come in handy now?

"You're Not Gonna Like This"

◆ SCENARIO ◆

Your protagonist and her lover have been traveling for days. They take a short break to rest and gather themselves, and the love interest decides to go out on his own to investigate what's ahead. When he comes back, he has upsetting news for your protagonist.

◆ BRAINSTORM ◆

How many days have they been traveling? How hungry are they? Do they have rations left? What is their morale like? How are they doing physically? How much stamina do they have?

◆ WRITE ◆

Write a scene where the love interest tells your protagonist they've reached an impasse. There is a cliff up ahead or a treacherous body of water or an impenetrable wall. Proceeding will require an act of great bravery—anything from making a big leap (if it's the cliff) or diving in headfirst (if it's the water) or scaling great heights (if it's the wall). What will they do?

◆ OPTIONAL ELEMENTS TO INCLUDE ◆

- Torn clothing.
- A wild animal appears at the worst possible moment.
- They lose a valuable item.

Fantasy Twist

What if your protagonist has special powers that have shut down because she is so exhausted? In this moment of dire need, can she find the strength to access her powers?

"On the Bright Side, We're Dead"

◆ SCENARIO ◆

Your main characters are stranded on an uninhabited planet. At first, they thought they weren't alone, but the longer they're out here, the clearer their solitude becomes. Their resources are dwindling. It looks like they're going to die out here. But at least they have each other, right?

◆ BRAINSTORM ◆

What do they miss about home? If they could send messages to their loved ones, who would they reach out to and what would they say? Think about the various ways they've found home in each other and how they would describe this relationship to the people who know them best.

◆ WRITE ◆

Write a scene where your protagonist and her lover give up on the idea of going home. Explore the idea that letting go of hope is good because it allows them to be present and enjoy the time they have left. How much joy and fun can they milk out of their last days together?

Remember: Just because they've accepted their fate doesn't mean they're correct. They might still get out of here. They might not even be alone! Depending on where this scene takes place in your story, quite a bit of adventure awaits them.

◆ OPTIONAL ELEMENTS TO INCLUDE ◆

- A prayer to a higher power.
- They talk about a food they miss.
- A mirage in the distance.

Fantasy Twist

What if the planet has feelings? It might not even want them here! Is there anything the planet might do to try to get rid of them? What if it's slowly poisoning them, causing hallucinations, or creating hazards in the landscape that make it unsafe to go anywhere?

Callbacks

Now that they've accepted their fate, does it make them wistful? Do they look back on the more difficult parts of their journey with fondness and perhaps a newfound sense of humor?

Quick Writes

Set a timer for 15 minutes and do not stop writing until the timer goes off. Do not edit, cross out, or censor yourself. Write down every thought that comes to you.

1. Write a scene where your protagonist is offered the only remaining seat on a rescue ship. But taking it would mean leaving her lover behind. What does she do?

2. Your protagonist makes a romantic meal using fruit and plants she's scavenged. Write a scene where her love interest has an allergic reaction to the food. How does she save him?

3. Write a scene where your protagonist and her lover lie under the stars, talking about the dreams they'll have to give up on if they never get rescued.

4. Your protagonist has been kidnapped by a violent group of intergalactic thieves and madmen. Write a scene where one honorable (and stunningly handsome?) thief makes a great sacrifice to help her escape.

5. Your protagonist is alone and lost at sea. Write a scene where she discovers someone else with her on the vessel. Where did he come from? Can she trust him?

TRADING PLACES

Your protagonist makes a pact with someone: I'll be you and you can be me. It might be identical twins switching places because they envy their sibling's lifestyle. Or maybe two characters were both in disfiguring accidents and they want a fresh start, so they swap nameplates on their hospital beds. Or two strangers accidentally cross paths while teleporting and end up in the other person's body.

Before Trading Places, these characters have plenty of preconceived notions about the path they didn't choose. The life they didn't end up living.

This little switcheroo gives them a chance to start over and find out if the grass really is greener. Ultimately, they get to decide if they had it better before, or if they prefer this new way of living.

But the real fun of a Trading Places story is that your joint protagonists end up connecting with people they never would've met in their former lives. They will find potential mates they never even would have spoken to before. It's like reaching the end of your Bumble matches and discovering another app that offers a smorgasbord of possible love interests. Or better yet, think of Trading Places as the opening of a portal to a whole new world of romantic adventures.

"There's One Thing You Need to Know"

◆ SCENARIO ◆

Your protagonist trades places with a long-lost twin who seems to have everything—an amazing home, tons of money, and a huge friend group. But just after they officially make their switch, the twin delivers bad news: "Someone wants me dead. Have fun being me!"

◆ BRAINSTORM ◆

Why would your protagonist give up her old life? Why did she think her twin had it so much easier? Investigate what her twin is running from and think about how your protagonist might respond.

◆ WRITE ◆

Write the scene after your protagonist discovers her new identity puts her in danger. Her long-gone twin didn't give her much information, so she must find out who wants her twin dead and why. It can't be this handsome stud who says he's her boyfriend, can it?

Remember: Your protagonist doesn't have any way of proving she isn't her twin. She can't just go back to her old life. She's stuck here in this new life, with these new problems.

◆ OPTIONAL ELEMENTS TO INCLUDE ◆

- A mysterious tattoo.
- A chest of jewels.
- A poisoned rose.

Fantasy Twist

Maybe it isn't a "who" on the hunt for your protagonist. What if it's a supernatural force? Something she will feel but can't see.

"You Better Not Destroy My Body"

◆ SCENARIO ◆

Your protagonist wakes up in someone else's home. She's confused at first. Then she looks in a mirror and suddenly this is worse than she thought because: "That's not my face, or my body!" Oh my God, she hasn't even had her morning coffee yet and already today's gone off the rails!

◆ BRAINSTORM ◆

What would you do if you woke up in someone else's body? We've seen and read plenty of body swap stories, so how can you reinvent this trope? How could your protagonist react in a way that feels fresh? Think about her belief system too—is this something she'd get used to quickly, or would it take her a while to accept the fact that this is real and not a dream?

◆ WRITE ◆

Write a scene where your protagonist calls or gets a call from home. (This could also be a FaceTime or a means of communication you create for your story, such as a Hologram Call.) She and this other person discover this is a body swap situation. Who knows how it happened—but as they talk, they realize it's a blessing. Neither one is in a rush to get back to their old rut. They decide to see what happens and check back with each other later. Your protagonists' first order of business? It's time to meet their new husbands . . .

◆ OPTIONAL ELEMENTS TO INCLUDE ◆

- Their new bodies are allergic to something unexpected.
- Their senses are heightened.
- Along with their new bodies come new physical turn-ons.

Fantasy Twist

Think about the rules of this supernatural event. Something must have triggered the body swap. If you want both characters to go back into the "correct" bodies at the end of your story, you'll need to decide how this happened so they can reverse it. Of course, they might decide not to go back.

Callbacks

Establish a literal "call back" agreement: Whenever your protagonists get in trouble or need help navigating a problem in the other person's life, they're only a phone call away. That doesn't mean the other person will always answer.

" I'll Do It If You Will "

◆ SCENARIO ◆

Your protagonist meets her doppelgänger. They get drunk together. They vent about their problems. They realize they can help each other. If they trade places, no one will ever know. They look enough alike that they could get away with doing the hard things they're afraid to do for themselves.

◆ BRAINSTORM ◆

Come up with a list of problems for both characters. From little things (like confronting a difficult boss) to more difficult challenges (like initiating a breakup or divorce) to terrible and bloody issues (like murder). Think about what's stopping them from fixing their own problems. Be as specific as possible with any justifications you come up with, as that may help your character's doppelgänger explain things later.

◆ WRITE ◆

Write a scene where your protagonist is getting ready to do something bad for her doppelgänger when she's surprised by her doppelgänger's partner/spouse/boyfriend/lover. This isn't what she's here for! But dear God, they're a charming, sexy distraction. She shouldn't. She really shouldn't. But they just . . . Oh no. She can't resist.

◆ OPTIONAL ELEMENTS TO INCLUDE ◆

- An unusual, nontraditional weapon.
- A kiss that keeps going and going and going and going . . .
- Your protagonist says something her doppelgänger would never say.

Fantasy Twist

Your protagonist thinks she's met her doppelgänger by chance, but what if there's something more sinister at work here? What if her doppelgänger isn't even a doppelgänger? What if this "twin" is secretly a shifter? And what if your protagonist's new love interest knows?

Callbacks

When your protagonist meets her doppelgänger, she learns about this person's life. She might have to use information from this conversation later to prove she is who she says she is.

Quick Writes

Set a timer for 15 minutes and do not stop writing until the timer goes off. Do not edit, cross out, or censor yourself. Write down every thought that comes to you.

1. Your impoverished protagonist trades places with someone who's swimming in money. Write a scene where her excess spending attracts the interest of a cute security guard.

2. Your human protagonist trades places with a mysterious traveling stranger. Write a scene where she discovers she's joined a band of supernatural ne'er-do-wells.

3. Write a scene where someone accuses your protagonist of not being who she says she is. She's forced to take a polygraph test (or a truth serum).

4. Write a scene where your protagonist thinks she sees her long-lost twin and pursues them, but they get away. Was it just her imagination?

5. Write a scene where your protagonist is enjoying a lazy, sexy weekend with her lover. Everything's going great. Until her lover accuses her of not being who she says she is.

Acknowledgments

My deepest thanks: To everyone at Simon & Schuster and Adams Media, especially my wonderful editor, Natalie McGregor (every step of this process has been a delight) and my fantastic development editor, Jennifer Kristal; to my entertainment lawyer, Mitch Smelkinson, for your "only the best" perspective; to Byrd Leavell, for your time and advice; to The Splinters, for giving me a writing home in all your living rooms; to Liza Palmer, Sarah Kuhn, and Amber Benson, for the crash course in traditional publishing and a million hours of side-by-side writing time; to everyone on TikTok asking for writing prompts; to Eleanor, Seth, and Drex, for the Friday night dinners full of love that fill my creative cup; and most of all, to Sherry Angel, for your notes, your guidance, and for making me want to be a writer in the first place.